TRUST

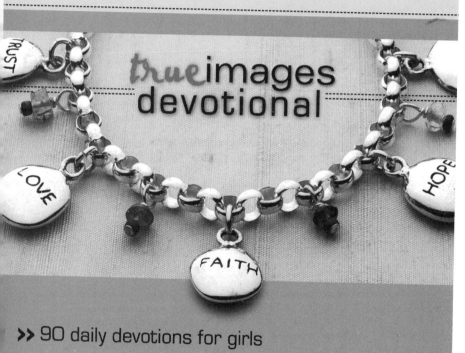

*true*images
devotional

LOVE

HOPE

FAITH

>> 90 daily devotions for girls

invert

trueimages
devotional

Amber Rae and Paige Drygas

ZONDERVAN™

GRAND RAPIDS, MICHIGAN 49530 USA

ZONDERVAN.COM/
AUTHORTRACKER

Youth Specialties

www.youthspecialties.com

True Images Devotional
Copyright © 2005 by The Livingstone Corporation

Youth Specialties products, 300 South Pierce Street, El Cajon, CA 92020, are published
by Zondervan, 5300 Patterson Avenue SE, Grand Rapids, MI 49530

Library of Congress Cataloging-in-Publication Data

True images devotional : 90 daily devotions for girls.
    p. cm.
  ISBN-10: 0-310-26705-6 (pbk.)
  ISBN-13: 978-0-310-26705-8 (pbk.)
  1. Teenage girls--Religious life. 2. Devotional calendars. I. Youth Specialties
(Organization)

BV4860. T78 2006
242'.633--dc22
                                                          2005024429

Produced with the assistance of *Livingstone* (www.LivingstoneCorp.com).
Project staff includes Paige Drygas, Mary Horner Collins, and Amber Rae.

*Creative team: Dave Urbanski, Heather Haggerty, Anna Hammond,
and SharpSeven Design
Cover design by Holly Sharp
Printed in the United States of America*

06 07 08 09 10 • 10 9 8 7 6 5 4 3 2 1

Contents

Welcome!

Are you wondering if this book is for you? Take the following quiz to find out.

Check all that apply. *You want...*

- ☐ To find a ready-made daily devotional tool.
- ☐ To develop the habit of spending time with God every day.
- ☐ To see God grow your faith over the next 90 days.
- ☐ To develop true, lasting, inner beauty (which means *character,* not appearance!).
- ☐ To see how God's Word relates to the issues in your life.
- ☐ To find a cool companion to *True Images: The Bible for Teen Girls.*
- ☐ To discover something challenging to read in your devotions.

If you checked one or more boxes above, then this is the book for you! The *True Images Devotional* includes 90 devotions written specifically for teenage girls. These devotions reflect the realities of life today (no glossing over the hard or ugly issues) and challenge you to make a statement—not about what you do or don't do, but about *who you are.*

Here's the set-up: The devotions are arranged in 13 topical sections. Scan the Contents page to get a quick idea of what's inside.

Each day's devotion fills two pages. You'll read an opening verse, a devotion on a character trait or issue, and a Bible passage. After you finish reading the Bible passage and the devotion, use the prayer starter to jumpstart your conversation with God for the day. Then utilize the journaling space at the end to write out your prayers, record your prayer requests (and God's answers), jot down what God is teaching you, whatever.

Any relationship takes time, doesn't it? You don't ignore your best friend for three months and then expect to pick up right back where you left off. Relationships take work. You have to invest in them. Your relationship with God is no exception. With all that you have going on in life, it can be easy to neglect your relationship with God. But it's your MIR (most important relationship). The purpose of this devotional is to connect you with God and connect God's Word with your life. That's where the power is!

So why are you still reading the lousy welcome page? Turn to the first devotion and go spend some time with God!

Amber Paige

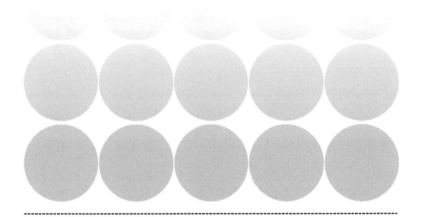

Section 1

Your Most Important Relationship

Not a "Family Plan"

Choose for yourselves this day whom you will serve.

Joshua 24:15b

If you've grown up around Christianity, you most likely know all the "right" things to say and do. "Read your Bible, go to church, say your prayers, be a good girl." Maybe it's easy for you to go with the flow and make it look like you belong to God. But do you really?

Contrary to popular opinion, growing up around Christians or going to church doesn't automatically make you a Christian. Knowing God is not like joining a cell phone company. God doesn't offer a "family share plan." He doesn't let you tag along and get "free minutes" because of the ones your parents have already paid for. God wants you to choose to serve him for yourself—not because of your parents, or your sister, or your friends. He wants you to do it because *you* want to!

John the Baptist spent some time with people who thought they were part of a "salvation family share plan." They figured that since Abraham had an "in" with God, and they were his descendants, then they were cool with God, too. But John was quick to tell them that salvation's not about your family's relationship with God; it's about *your* relationship with God.

You see, no one else can choose Christianity for you. You have to choose to love and follow Jesus for yourself. It's the most important choice you will ever make. It's the most important relationship you can ever have. While your relationships with friends, guys, family, teachers, and youth leaders are all significant and valuable, your relationship with God is more important than all of those combined. It's the one relationship that *should* define who you are on earth and that *will* determine how you spend eternity. So choose for yourself this day—whom will *you* serve?

 READ FOR YOURSELF WHAT JOHN THE BAPTIST HAD TO SAY ABOUT CHOOSING TO FOLLOW GOD IN LUKE 3:1-18.

 God, I want to know you for myself. Show me what it means to serve you each and every day—not because of what anyone else does, but because I want to love you on my own...

You're Invited

Come, all you who are thirsty, come to the waters;...Listen, listen to me, and eat what is good, and your soul will delight in the richest of fare.

Isaiah 55:1a, 2b

Surely it's happened to you. You go to the fridge looking for something to munch on, trying to satisfy a craving. You open the door and stare. All the good stuff's gone. Your options are stale bread, moldy cheese, unidentifiable leftovers, and bags of frozen vegetables. Yuck!

Can you imagine if just at that moment your best friend called with this invitation: "Hey, my mom's practicing for her gourmet cooking class. She just made an outrageous spread! We're having shrimp cocktail, bruschetta, Caesar salad, filet mignon, and an amazing chocolate truffle cheesecake for dessert. Get over here and help me eat all this!" Hmmm, fridge or friend's house—which would you choose? What a no-brainer!

Did you realize that your soul has similar options? Deep down we all crave something more than what this life offers. We search for meaning. We ache to belong. And we try to satisfy those longings on our own—through relationships with guys, friends, partying, sports, academics, looking good, or having the coolest clothes and stuff. But those things are like stale bread and moldy cheese—they will never satisfy your cravings.

Meanwhile God invites you to come to an incredible, all-you-can-eat gourmet banquet for your soul! You don't need to worry about what to wear, what to say, or how to act. You only need to come, just the way you are. Your spot at the banquet table is paid for and reserved (courtesy of Jesus). Come and enjoy God's never-ending supply of hope, help, comfort, love, wisdom, strength—the menu goes on and on. Every good thing imaginable is there for the taking. How will you RSVP to God's invitation?

 READ ISAIAH 55:1-13 FOR MORE ABOUT GOD'S INVITATION TO YOU.

 Father, thanks for making it possible for me to come to you. Forgive me for the ways I've tried to satisfy my soul on my own. I accept your invitation to come to you for a feast for my soul...

Forget the Rules

Woe to you, teachers of the law and Pharisees, you hypocrites!
You are like whitewashed tombs, which look beautiful on the
outside but on the inside are full of dead men's bones and
everything unclean. In the same way, on the outside you appear to
people as righteous but on the inside you are full of hypocrisy and
wickedness.

Matthew 23:27-28

Harsh words from Jesus! In these verses Jesus describes the Jewish religious leaders (a.k.a. "the Pharisees"). These guys *so* did not get the point. They thought they could impress God by following a heavy-duty list of rules, which they had made up themselves. They went to a lot of effort to look very spiritual on the outside. To them, that was what mattered most.

But on several occasions Jesus told them they had it all wrong. He told them that instead of following all their little rules they'd made up, they needed to focus on following God's most important command: to love God with all your heart and with all your soul and with all your mind (Matthew 22:37). See, being a Christian is really about what's on the inside. It's about having an intense, real, all-consuming relationship with God. It's about loving him with every part of who you are. Of course, God does have things he wants you to do or not do—but he wants you to obey him out of love and gratitude, not out of a sense of duty. That goes a whole lot deeper than a list of rules, don't you think?

Let's talk about you now. Do you give God lip service that's empty of passion and meaning? Do you call yourself a Christian while your heart is far from God? Do you consider yourself a "good Christian" just because you don't swear, smoke, or drink? Don't be like the Pharisees who missed the point. God wants so much more from you than following some checklist of do's and don'ts. He wants all of you—heart, soul, and mind.

 WANT TO SEE JUST HOW UNIMPRESSED JESUS WAS BY THE PHARISEES AND THEIR RULES? READ THE WHOLE FIERY STORY IN MATTHEW 23:13-39.

 *God, I don't want to miss the point of what it means to be a Christian. Show me what it means to love you with all my heart, with all my soul, and with all my mind...*

Extreme Makeover

"How to get that guy to notice you!"

"Try our ultimate makeover!"

"Test your fashion know-how!"

"The prom workout that will transform your body!"

The headlines of a typical magazine tend to focus on you, you, you. But here's a little secret: It's not all about you.

What's not all about you? *Life. Eternity. Everything.* It's not about you; it's about the one who created you. It's about knowing that the Lord is God, and you're not. It's about obeying the Master, since you're the servant. It's about trusting the Shepherd, since he knows how to perfectly love, protect, guide, and care for his sheep.

Talk about a different way of looking at things. We're so used to focusing on ourselves 24-7. Don't you think it's time for a change?

Ask God to give you a perspective makeover. Ask him to transform your mind so that you spend the day focused on God and not on yourself. So that you concentrate more on what you can give to God than on what you can get from God. So that you thank God for all he's given you instead of focusing on what you don't have.

Wanna know another secret? When you focus less on you and more on God, amazing things happen. You become a much happier person. You have peace even in tough situations. You learn how to be content in all circumstances. Now those are the kind of makeover results that only God can produce!

 THE PSALMISTS KNEW WHAT IT MEANT TO TAKE THEIR EYES OFF THEMSELVES AND FIX THEM FIRMLY ON GOD. SEE THE RESULTS OF THEIR CHANGED PERSPECTIVES IN PSALM 95:1-7 AND PSALM 100.

>> *God, it's so easy for me to think about myself all day. Change my heart and my mind so that I think more about you and less about me. Teach me to focus on you—every moment of every day...*

Better Than Pilates

Train yourself to be godly. For physical training is of some value,
but godliness has value for all things, holding promise for both the
present life and the life to come.

1Timothy 4:7b-8

Studies show that regular exercise benefits your mind as well as your body. You look and feel better when you work out. "Amen!" says the apostle Paul. He agrees that there's real value in training yourself physically.

But—and that's the key word here!—it has limited value compared to training yourself spiritually. Working hard at spiritual fitness will benefit you not only for the next 70 years or so that you live on earth but also for all eternity.

Have you given much thought to your *spiritual* workout routine? Here are some tips for your "godliness training program."

Watch your diet. Be careful about what you feed your mind. Evaluate what kind of music, movies, television, books, and magazines you consume. Ask God to show you if those things are helping or hurting your spiritual health. And make sure God's Word is the staple of your diet.

Work hard. Just as jogging once a week isn't enough to keep you in shape physically, spending time with God just once a week isn't enough to keep you in shape spiritually. Regularly invest time and energy into knowing God.

Exercise. Start with stretching—be willing to obey, even when it's hard. Set an example of godliness even when others look down on you. Exercise your faith. Practice putting your hope in God. Look for opportunities to use the spiritual gifts God gave you.

Find a workout buddy. Surround yourself with others who also have the same workout goal: godliness. Training with others will motivate you to not give up!

As with any fitness program, you may feel overwhelmed about starting. Or you may start out enthusiastically but hit some slumps along the way. Don't be discouraged. Keep at it. Remember, it's worth it in the long run!

 For a more complete description of Paul's suggested training routine, read 1 Timothy 4:6-16.

 God, help me to work hard at godliness. Show me how to value the health of my spirit even more than I do the health of my body...

So Much to Say

A lot of girls never read the Bible. They think, *Why bother? It's hard to
understand. It's written for old people. It doesn't relate to my life today. I
doubt I'm missing much.*

But *you* know better, right? You know the Bible's more than an
ordinary bunch of words. It holds the words of God himself. In any
relationship, you have to listen to the other person in order to really
know that person. If you're going to get to know God, then you have
to listen to what he says. Don't assume you already know everything
there is to know about God, because you can't! God is so big that
you'll never reach the end of him. There's always something new to
discover about him, and the best way to get to know God is through
his Word.

Once you dig in, you'll find that the Bible really does have a lot
to say about the things that matter most to you. You want to know
what God says about sex? About reacting to mean girls at school?
About what to do when someone rejects you or betrays your trust?
About feeling alone and unloved? About how to deal with life when
it seems totally out of control? Just take a good look in your Bible.

Do you wonder how to dress, how to talk, how to act? How to make choices about your future? How to treat your friends and your family? It's all in there.

You don't have to stumble through life unsure of what to do. God isn't aloof. He's not standoffish. He's available for you to get to know him, anytime. So, what are you waiting for? Dive into God's Word and start discovering who he is for yourself!

 Check out the words of someone who truly loved God's Word in Psalm 119:161-176.

 God, I want to know you more. Help me to make the most of the opportunities you've given me to know you through your Word...

In Case of Emergency

Do not be anxious about anything, but in everything, by prayer and petition, with thanksgiving, present your requests to God.

Philippians 4:6

Say your dad loses his job, and you'll probably have to move—what's your *first* response? Say your best friend comes to you and tells you she might be pregnant—what's your *first* response? Say your biology teacher's all over your case because you questioned evolution—what's your *first* response? Say a gang member at school gets in your face because she doesn't "like your attitude"—what's your *first* response?

A. Get on the phone with your best friend and talk about the problem from every angle. After all, isn't that what friends are for?

B. Ask *all* your friends, one after another, for their advice on what to do. Take an informal poll. Isn't that what politicians do?

C. Keep it to yourself. Mull it over, consider all possible solutions and solve it on your own. Isn't that the responsible thing to do?

D. Deny it. Pretend the problem doesn't exist. Don't think about it. Eventually everything will work itself out, right?

Which option did you pick? While answers A through D are all pretty natural responses, God wants us to take a more supernatural approach to the crises we face. He wants us to turn to him first. He wants to be the one we run to when life hurts. He wants us to pray *as soon as the problem comes up*—not after we exhaust our own solutions.

King Hezekiah did it God's way. When faced with possible annihilation from an enemy army, Hezekiah immediately poured his heart out to God. His first response was to take his problem to God in prayer. He didn't convene an emergency military meeting. He didn't call his friends. He didn't map out evacuation routes. He went straight to God. Next time trouble comes your way, where will you turn first?

 FOR THE WHOLE STORY OF WHAT HAPPENED WHEN HEZEKIAH TURNED TO GOD IN PRAYER, READ ISAIAH 37:14-37.

 God, remind me to turn to you first when hard things happen in my day. Help me to remember who you are and to trust you to solve my problems...

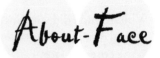

About-Face

Repent, then, and turn to God, so that your sins may be wiped out,
that times of refreshing may come from the Lord.

Acts 3:19

You catch a friend in a lie, and she says she's sorry. But the next day,
she lies to you again. Once more, you accept her apology. Now if on
the third day she lies *again,* will you believe her when she says she's
sorry? Probably not. Will you be satisfied with her apology? Probably
not. That's because what you really need from your friend isn't a routine apology; it's repentance.

Repentance. It's one of those fancy theological words you hear
at church. But what exactly does it mean? *Repentance* means that you
realize you're heading in the wrong direction—acting and thinking
a certain way—and then you do a 180-degree turn and head in the
exact opposite direction. It means doing an "about-face" and doing
things God's way instead of your way. It means being sorry enough
about your actions to want to change them. And just like you want
your friend to offer you more than an insincere "I'm sorry," God
wants more from you when you sin against him. He wants sincere
repentance.

Do you have an area in your life where you need to repent?
Maybe you're going further with your boyfriend than you know you

should. Maybe you're deceiving your parents by only telling them part of the story. Maybe you have a habit of saying some catty things about other girls to make you feel better about yourself or to look cool in front of your friends.

Whatever the issue is, it's time for an about-face. Confess your sin to God and ask for forgiveness. Ask God to give you a sincere sorrow over your sin that will cause you to turn from it. And know that when you do, God will wipe out that sin completely, and you'll experience how refreshing it is to have your relationship with God back on track.

 FOR AN EXAMPLE OF AN HONEST PRAYER OF GENUINE REPENTANCE, READ PSALM 32.

 Dear God, I don't want to keep blowing off my sin. Help me to have true sorrow that leads to real repentance. Forgive me for my sin and restore my relationship with you...

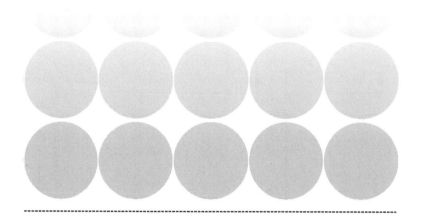

Section 2

God's Identity

A Love That Lasts

But from everlasting to everlasting the LORD's love is with those
who fear him.

Psalm 103:17a

As little girls we put Ken and Barbie in their dream house to live
happily together forever and wondered what it would be like to be
Barbie and find our own dream guy. We watched Prince Charming
rescue Cinderella from her wicked stepmother to live happily ever
after in his castle and wondered if there might someday be a Prince
Charming for us.

A love that lasts forever. A guy you can count on to love you, no
matter what. Isn't that what every girl dreams of finding?

As we grow up, somehow that dream persists. No matter how
much a girl likes to flirt or play the field, deep down she wants to
find one guy who will love her forever. She longs for a relationship
with depth and meaning, for a love that is strong and enduring. She
wants to spend her life with the perfect guy who will love her with a
perfect love.

Someday you may find a guy who will love you for as long as you
both shall live—a great guy who will love you to the best of his abil-
ity. But no guy can ever love you with a perfect love, because no guy

is perfect. Only God is perfect, and only his love is perfect. If you're looking for a love that will last forever—guaranteed—the only place you'll find that is in God.

When you find yourself longing for a guy in your life, when you feel the desire to be swept off your feet and loved and cherished, turn to God. God put the desire to love and to be loved in your heart, but he wants you to find that fulfilled first and foremost in him. Let your relationship with God be the first and greatest romance of your life.

 LEARN MORE ABOUT GOD AND HIS EVERLASTING LOVE FOR YOU IN PSALM 103.

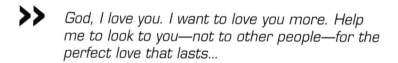 *God, I love you. I want to love you more. Help me to look to you—not to other people—for the perfect love that lasts...*

Just as You Are

The LORD did not set his affection on you and choose you because you were more numerous than other peoples, for you were the fewest of all peoples. But it was because the LORD loved you.

Deuteronomy 7:7-8a

Deep down we all want to be accepted. Whose acceptance do you crave most? (Pick the following that best describes you.)

1. *Your parents.* You work hard to be their dream child, follow their rules, and help out around the house. You want to excel at what you do so they'll be proud of you.

2. *Your friends.* You make sure your clothes are in style, and you want your friends to envy you. You have a certain attitude that you know will impress them.

3. *Guys.* You diet, work out, and make sure you look good so you can win their attention. And since guys seem to want someone who's funny, smart, sexy, thin, sassy, and confident, you do your best to be all that and more.

4. *Your coach or teacher.* You practice extra hard at your sport so you can make your coach proud. You work hard in school for outstanding grades. You work harder at your music/drama/art than anyone else so your teacher will be proud of you.

Wouldn't it be great to be loved and accepted just as you are, without having to try to impress anyone? Believe it or not—you are! God didn't choose the Israelites because of anything special they'd done; he chose them simply because he loved them. The same is true with you—God loves you simply because he wants to. You can't earn his love; *therefore you can't lose his love.* He accepts you just as you are.

Realizing that God knows and loves the real you sets you free to be yourself. So quit trying so hard to impress everybody. God accepts you, and that's what matters most.

GOD CHOOSES TO LOVE US AND WANTS US TO ENJOY A SPECIAL RELATIONSHIP WITH HIM. LEARN MORE ABOUT THE RELATIONSHIP GOD WANTED TO HAVE WITH ISRAEL IN DEUTERONOMY 7:1-16.

God, I can't believe you know the real me and still choose to love me. Help me to find the confidence to be myself with others because you already accept me...

The Perfect Hideout

Trust in him at all times, O people; pour out your hearts to him, for God is our refuge.

Psalm 62:8

Have you ever had one of those days when you just didn't want to get out of bed and face reality? You'd prefer to hide out under the covers. You hope that when you do eventually come out, your life will somehow have self-corrected.

What things make you want to hide from life? Maybe you embarrassed yourself in front of your crush. Maybe you had a fight with a friend or parent. Maybe someone at school enjoys making you feel miserable. Maybe you feel unsure of yourself, awkward and out of place. Maybe your parents are constantly fighting, and you want to escape the tension. Maybe you live with abuse—verbal, physical, or sexual.

What do you do when you just want to disappear from life for a while? Do you look for a haven in your friends or family? Go to a guy to make you feel safe and protected? Use drugs or alcohol to attempt to escape? Trust in your own talents and abilities? Turn into a perfectionist and attempt to control every possible detail of life? Try to comfort yourself through food—either by eating too much or by showing how much control you can exercise by not eating at all?

While those things may provide a temporary sense of security, they are—at best—flimsy shelters to stand under. God is the only real refuge, the only hiding place you can really trust to protect you during the storms of life. Psalm 62:8 offers some solid advice on dealing with the low points of life: trust God; pour out your problems to him; take refuge in the only perfect hideout.

 READ THE PRAYER OF A MAN WHO FOUND REFUGE IN GOD IN PSALM 62.

>> *God, there are so many times when I just want to hide from my life. Thank you for being my refuge. Help me to turn to you whenever I need help. Remind me to pour out my heart to you when things get tough...*

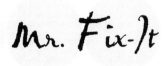

Mr. Fix-It

Therefore this is what the Lord says: "If you repent, I will restore you that you may serve me."

Jeremiah 15:19a

You blew it. You gave away your virginity. You lied and sneaked out of the house. You got wasted and made an absolute fool of yourself at a party. You experimented with homosexuality. Shoplifted. Did drugs. Drove drunk and hurt somebody.

The worst part is that you knew better. You knew what God wanted from you, but you turned your back on him and did your own thing anyway. And now you wonder if God could ever forgive you. You figure he has every reason to write you off.

Here comes the good news: God is in the restoration business. He can fix what you broke, and he can rebuild what you tore down. If you confess your sin to him, if you're sorry enough to turn from it, then he promises to restore you. It's what he does! God never turns his back on anyone who comes to him for forgiveness. His grace and his mercy can't be measured, and his love and compassion have no end.

Just ask Peter. Though he swore to always follow Jesus, to even die for him, when things got tough, Peter abandoned Jesus. Peter even went so far as to deny he even knew Jesus—not once, not twice, but three times! Peter knew the devastation of really blowing it. But he also knew the sweetness of God's restoration. Jesus forgave Peter and restored their relationship. He gave Peter an important job in his kingdom.

No matter how great your sin, God's grace and mercy are greater. His forgiveness is there for the asking. Confess, turn to him, and let God restore you.

 For the full story of Peter's denial and restoration read John 13:31-38, 18:15-27, and 21:15-19.

 God, I messed up—really, really messed up. I know it, and I know that you know it. I'm so sorry. Please forgive my sin and restore my relationship with you...

So Close

Where can I go from your Spirit? Where can I flee from your presence?

Psalm 139:7

Have you ever had that all-alone feeling, even in the middle of a crowd? Even surrounded by a dozen friends, it's possible to feel terribly lonely.

Though your feelings might be telling you that you're on your own, you can't always trust your feelings. The truth is that you are never alone. God is always with you. No matter where you go, no matter what you do, no matter how you feel—you are not alone. God is there.

King David knew a lot about loneliness. He often felt alone and deserted. But he knew that those feelings weren't to be trusted, and he chose to trust instead in what he knew to be true about God. In Psalm 139 he reminds himself—and us—of these truths: God knows every detail of your life. He knows everything you do, everything you think, everything you feel. Even before you say a word, God knows exactly what it will be.

Do you realize that you could never get away from God if you tried? Not a single place exists where God's Spirit is not present. Even if you attempted to get away from God, it's just not possible. He is always, always, always with you—even when it doesn't feel like it.

God cares about the little things and the big things in your life. He cares about how you did on a test and the divorce your parents are going through and how much it hurt when your boyfriend broke up with you. Through every moment of every day—whether seemingly unimportant or clearly a big deal—don't ever forget that God is with you.

 READ PSALM 139:1-10 AND BE ENCOURAGED BY DAVID'S REMINDER THAT GOD IS ALWAYS WITH YOU.

 God, thank you that even when I feel alone, I'm really not. Remind me that you're with me at all times. Teach me to focus on the truth that I'm never truly on my own, because you're always there, too...

Let's Party!

A man can do nothing better than to eat and drink and find satisfaction in his work. This too, I see, is from the hand of God, for without him, who can eat or find enjoyment?

Ecclesiastes 2:24-25

God wants you to be a party girl. What? That can't be! But it's true. God wants you to enjoy life, each and every day he's given you. All the good things you experience come from his hand, and they're meant to be enjoyed as gifts from him. They're meant to point you to the Giver.

Many people think of God as the "cosmic killjoy"—out to ruin all their fun with his rules. No getting drunk, no doing drugs, no sex until marriage, etc. They think such prohibitions take all the fun out of life. But when God says "No," what he really means is "Don't hurt yourself." God knows that such short-term pleasures will never satisfy your thirst. In fact, they only make you thirstier.

We all long to truly enjoy life. But true joy can only be found in a relationship with God. And it will only be found when we recognize him in the gifts that he gives—and enjoy those gifts in the way he intended.

Solomon, the writer of Ecclesiastes, was the authority on this subject. He spent a lot of time trying to enjoy God's gifts apart from God himself. Solomon had all the wealth, power, money, prestige, women, and sex that a guy could want. And while it brought short-term excitement, it failed to bring lasting joy. In the end, Solomon concluded that all those things were meaningless and empty apart from God.

So go on, enjoy all the good things life has to offer—but recognize where those things come from (God). Find your ultimate satisfaction in your relationship with him. And enjoy those things the way he intended you to.

 FOR MORE OF SOLOMON'S CONCLUSIONS ON ENJOYING LIFE, READ ECCLESIASTES 11:7-12:1 AND 12:13-14.

 God, help me to enjoy life and the good things you give me...but to always see past those things to you—the Giver. Help me to be a girl who finds her joy ultimately in you...

Super-Daddy

> But you received the Spirit of sonship.
> And by him we cry, "Abba, Father."
>
> Romans 8:15b

Picking out a Father's Day card can be a tricky ordeal. If your dad's warm, loving, protective, and always there for you, then it's not so hard. But greeting cards don't seem to have much to say for mean or abusive dads. For dads so caught up in their own stuff they don't pay much attention to you. For controlling or negative dads. And sadly, many of us don't have a great "greeting card" kind of dad. At least not here on earth.

But did you know that when you became a Christian, you became a child of God? You received the Spirit of sonship (or in your case, "daughtership"). God became your "Abba"—that means "Daddy" in Aramaic. Because of God's Spirit in you, God is your Daddy.

God is the most perfect dad imaginable. If you have an A-Okay earthly dad, God is infinitely better! And if you've got a not-so-great dad, then know that God's nothing like him. Instead, he's the dad you always dreamed of having. He always knows what to say. He's always there for you. He always protects you and guides you. You can count on him to never leave you. He watches over you and cares for you, no matter what. He loves you, and he's proud of you just the way you are. Those sappy-perfect TV dads can't even begin to compare with him.

So when life's going great, and you want someone to share that with, turn to your Daddy and tell him all about it. When life stinks and you just want someone to hold you and make it all better, turn to your Daddy and spill out all your hurts on him. He sacrificed everything in order to make you his daughter. Make the most of being your Daddy's girl!

 FOR MORE ON BOTH THE PRIVILEGES AND RESPONSIBILITIES OF BEING A CHILD OF GOD, READ ROMANS 8:1-17.

 God, thank you for all you did to make me your daughter. Thank you for being the perfect dad. Teach me more of what it means to be your child...

Expect the Unexpected

Now Naaman was commander of the army of the king of Aram...He was a valiant soldier, but he had leprosy.

2 Kings 5:1

Ever feel like an outcast? Like there's something so seriously wrong with you that nobody wants to have anything to do with you? Well, Naaman was a true-blue outcast. He had an incurable disease called *leprosy,* and lepers were usually isolated from the rest of society to keep their disease from spreading.

Good thing Naaman got hooked up with Elisha, God's prophet. Elisha sent a messenger to tell Naaman that he would be healed if he washed himself seven times in the Jordan River. You'd think Naaman would be excited about this. Ecstatic even. But nooooo. He actually got ticked off. He'd expected to be healed in some flashy way, and this washing-in-a-river thing seemed so basic, so mundane. He almost blew off the whole thing. But fortunately for him he decided to give it a try—and he was healed!

What's the point? The point is that sometimes we're like Naaman; we ask God for something, and we get upset when he doesn't answer the way we expected. You may ask God to heal a dying loved one, and instead God gives you strength to bear the pain of losing that person. You may hope for a friend, and God sends one in the form of a not-so-cool new girl. You may pray for people to like you, and God reminds you that he loves you.

Remember, God has his own way of doing things, and he's the one in charge. Instead of getting bent out of shape because God didn't answer the way you wanted, look for how he *did* answer. God knows what he's doing, and his way is best. Trust in whatever answer he gives you. Don't miss out on his blessings because they didn't come packaged the way you expected. Accept what he gives you and praise him for it.

 Check out the whole story of Naaman's healing in 2 Kings 5:1-16.

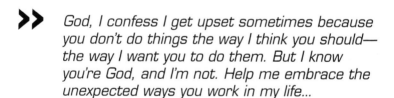 *God, I confess I get upset sometimes because you don't do things the way I think you should— the way I want you to do them. But I know you're God, and I'm not. Help me embrace the unexpected ways you work in my life...*

Show Some Respect

Charm is deceptive, and beauty is fleeting;
but a woman who fears the Lord is to be praised.

Proverbs 31:30

Imagine this: You're a lowly freshman; basically a nobody in your school. By some odd twist of fate, you end up sitting alone at lunch with *the* guy on campus. We're talking about the poster-boy for Mr. Tall, Dark, and Handsome. He's charming and oh-so cute. Student body president, varsity athlete in three sports, editor of the school paper—this guy does it all and has it all. And for some reason, he's decided to talk to you.

If you're like most girls, this would be an overwhelming experience. You'd feel thoroughly unprepared for this. Guys like *him* just don't talk to girls like *you*. You'd be too nervous to relax and be yourself. You'd be so in awe of this guy that you'd have a hard time talking. And you'd think everything he said was perfect.

Although this analogy doesn't even begin to come close, it describes a little bit of what it means to "fear the Lord." Fearing God means you recognize that he is far, far above you; that you're not at all in the same "class." It means you look up to him in wonder, amazed that he'd want to communicate with you at all. Far more than any person, God is infinitely worthy of your respect. He absolutely deserves to be feared, revered, honored, and admired. He's someone you can really look up to—way more than the world's most amazing guy.

And guess what happens when you fear the Lord? You grow more and more beautiful. Even the most attractive women grow old and are forgotten. No matter how beautiful they once were, their beauty just doesn't last. But when you fear God, you develop an inner beauty that doesn't fade with time. Your respect for God makes you beautiful, truly beautiful, no matter how old you become.

Don't take God lightly. Treat him with the respect he deserves. And watch how absolutely gorgeous you become.

 Discover more of what it means to fear the Lord in Proverbs 1:7, 2:1-5, 3:7, 8:13, 9:10, 14:27, 15:33, and 23:17.

 God, develop in me the kind of beauty that lasts forever. Increase my respect for you and show me more of what it means to fear you...

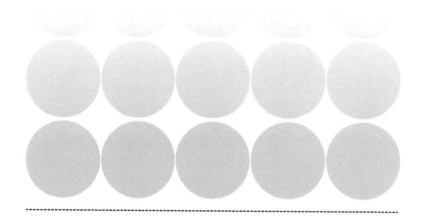

Section 3

The Beauty of Faith

What Are You Known For?

Now faith is being sure of what we hope for and certain of what we do not see. This is what the ancients were commended for.

Hebrews 11:1-2

If you died tomorrow, what would your obituary say? Not sure? Well, what are you known for? Your killer wardrobe? Your long, lush hair? Your infectious laugh? Your good grades? Your cool car? Your amazing athletic abilities? Your way with words? Your kindness to your friends?

What about your faith? Would that make it anywhere on the list?

Hebrews 11 talks about a bunch of remarkable people who were known for one thing: *faith*. Ordinary men and women such as Abel, Noah, Abraham, Sarah, Joseph, Moses, and Rahab (a prostitute) became extraordinary because of their faith.

Though they were all very different, these heroes of the faith had this in common: They set their hearts on what they couldn't see. Even though they couldn't see God, they believed in him. They were sure that God had something better than this world waiting for them. So they lived life on earth motivated by the dream of heaven. That faith gave them the courage to honor God even in horrible, horrible circumstances. And God applauded them for it. Can you imagine God standing and clapping for you?

Do you have a faith that pleases God? Do you live like your years on earth are all there is to life, or do you live with eternity in mind? You may not have to build an ark or lead God's people through the desert, but you do have to put God first throughout your day.

If you don't have that kind of faith yet, do you want it? God has all kinds of ways of growing your faith. And you can bet he's already started. Do whatever it takes to be known as a girl of faith. It's the best thing you could ever be known for.

 GET A BETTER LOOK AT THE KIND OF FAITH THAT GOD APPLAUDS BY READING HEBREWS 11.

 God, thank you that faith makes ordinary people like me extraordinary in your eyes. I want that kind of faith. I know my faith is weak, so please make it stronger...

When the Heat Is On

If we are thrown into the blazing furnace, the God we serve
is able to save us from it...But even if he does not, we want
you to know, O king, that we will not serve your gods or
worship the image of gold you have set up.

Daniel 3:17-18

When the going gets tough, the tough...*have faith*? That's right,
baby! Take a moment now and put yourself in the shoes of Shadrach,
Meshach, and Abednego. They've got an incredibly tough choice to
make: Be true to God and get tossed into a blazing furnace or just
quietly let this whole God-thing go and walk away burn-free. Which
would *you* choose?

Those young men chose to trust God. They faced the fire, knowing that God *could* save them from it—but that he might have a different plan. And they chose to keep the faith, either way.

It's easy to say you'd act in faith, but it can be awfully hard
when you're actually facing the fire. Though you're not likely to ever
get tossed into an actual furnace, you do face things in life that feel
pretty scary.

What do you fear? Speaking in public? Never finding true
love? Sharing your faith with the girls at school? Standing up for

creationism in your biology class? Getting raped? Getting shot? Are you afraid of heights? Scared your dad will leave? No matter what you face, you can trust God to take care of you. He can save you from any situation; and even if he chooses not to, you can still trust that he's in charge. Even in the furnace, he'll be with you.

When you follow God into the fire, your faith shines. Others will notice. They'll wonder how you do it. And that's when your faith shines brightest and brings God glory.

 Find encouragement in the full story of Shadrach, Meshach, and Abednego, who faced the fire in Daniel 3.

 God, even if I'm in a really scary situation, I know I can trust in you. Please make my faith shine for your glory...

The Waiting Game

Wait for the LORD; be strong and take heart and wait for the LORD.

Psalm 27:14

We get lots of practice at waiting. You have to wait to get your driver's license, wait for the results from tryouts, wait in line at amusement parks, wait for that certain guy to notice you, wait until you're old enough to be out on your own—the list goes on and on. In spite of all that practice, we're really not very good at waiting patiently, are we?

The bottom line is that we just don't like to wait. We want things now, *now,* ***now!*** Fast food, high-speed Internet, instant messaging, microwaves, digital cameras—so many things in our society feed our expectation that we can have what we want instantly. No waiting required.

Waiting can be especially hard when you're stuck in a difficult situation. Like when your parents talk about splitting up. Or when other students spread nasty rumors about you. Or when you try unsuccessfully to make friends in a new place. In painful situations, it's more difficult than ever to wait.

That's when we usually start looking for the quick fix, don't we? But sorry, Charlene, most of the time there's nothing you can do but wait it out. God knows your situation, but he's less concerned with the instant outcome than with what he wants you to learn in the process. It's time to keep waiting and start learning.

Waiting teaches you to lean on God. It helps your faith to grow. God doesn't just want you to wait. He wants you to wait *for him,* since he's the only one who can really make the difference. When you find yourself stuck some place you don't want to be, with no apparent way out, wait for God. He will make a way, in his time. Your patience will be rewarded. Guaranteed.

 DAVID WENT THROUGH LOADS OF HARD TIMES WHERE HE WAS FORCED TO WAIT ON GOD. READ PSALM 27 WHERE HE SHARES HOW HE FOUND HIS HOPE AND STRENGTH IN GOD AS HE WAITED ON HIM.

 God, you know how much I don't like to wait! It's hard to wait for you to act. Show me how to really lean on you as I wait and to learn what you want to teach me in the process...

Get with It!

Picture this: You arrive at school in shambles, wearing only one shoe, the same T-shirt you wore yesterday, and your pajama pants. Your hair is still all snarly from bed. You have makeup on just one eye and only one earring in. You run into class and discover that you lost your homework, and you have to do a presentation you totally forgot about. Then the guy you've had a crush on forever points out the toilet paper hanging from the leg of your pajama pants. (Yeah, that's the point where you wake up screaming!)

All right, so that's the stuff of bad dreams, not real life. Or is it? 'Fess up now. Don't you at least feel a *little* like that sometimes? Like you don't quite have it all together to face the challenges of the day?

Well, you're not alone. In his Gospel, Mark tells the story of a father who brought his son to Jesus for healing. When Jesus told him all things are possible (including healing) for those who believe, the man cried out, "I do believe; help me overcome my unbelief!" See? This guy didn't have it all together, either.

The father *wanted* to believe, but he knew he didn't believe like he ought to. So did he put on a brave front? Pretend to be more than he was? Try to impress Jesus with fake faith? No! He was honest with Jesus and with himself.

One of the many, many great things about God is that he doesn't care if you're not perfectly with it. He just cares that you bring him what you've got. That's because he's the great multiplier—taking the little you do have and making it grow.

Go on and be honest with God. It's okay to pray, "God, I love you—help me love you more. I trust you—help me trust you more. I believe in you—help me believe you more." And don't worry; he will.

 CHECK OUT THE WHOLE STORY OF THE NOT-ALL-TOGETHER DAD IN MARK 9:14-27.

 God, thanks that I don't have to be perfect. I'm so glad I can bring you what I've got and know that you'll supply what's missing. I believe, Father; help me overcome my unbelief...

Walk on the Wild Side

Then Peter got down out of the boat, walked on the water and came toward Jesus. But when he saw the wind, he was afraid and, beginning to sink, cried out, "Lord, save me!" Immediately Jesus reached out his hand and caught him. "You of little faith," he said, "why did you doubt?"

Matthew 14:29b-31

How cool is that! Peter actually got to walk on water! Imagine what a rush that must have been for him. He realized that Jesus was out on the water and wanted to join him. So he climbed out of that boat, stepped onto the water, and didn't go under. Wild! Amazing! Unforgettable! With each step Peter experienced the impossible. Can you just picture the expression on his face? Until...

He started paying more attention to the wind than to Jesus. Suddenly his brain started sending warning signs. *Oh Peter, you have no business being out here! You're gonna sink! Have you ever heard of a little thing called "drowning"?* Peter got frightened, began to doubt, and suddenly started sinking fast.

Can you relate to Peter? Has God asked you to step out in faith, but you find yourself focusing on all the things that can go wrong instead of on Jesus? Perhaps you know you need to break up with your non-Christian boyfriend, but you're worried you'll never find another guy. Or maybe you know you need to take a stand with your friends—to speak out against abortion, to support the existence of God, to share what the Bible says about homosexuality, to defend abstinence until marriage, or to affirm there's only one way to heaven—but you're scared you won't have any friends after you do. What can you do?

Do what Peter did when he started to sink: Call for help! Reach out to Jesus. He'll keep you from going under. Focus on Jesus and let him deal with everything else. The One who called you onto the water in the first place won't ever let you drown. Ignore your doubts and trust in him.

 READ THE WHOLE STORY OF PETER'S AMAZING "WALK ON THE WILD SIDE" IN MATTHEW 14:22-33.

 Jesus, I know you want me to step out in faith. But I confess that I'm scared. Help me keep my focus on you alone...

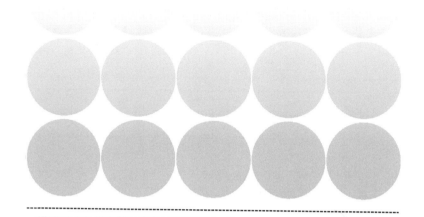

Section 4

When Life Hurts

Casting Away

Cast your cares on the LORD and he will sustain you;
he will never let the righteous fall.

Psalm 55:22

Try this little experiment: Check out the list of Top 40 songs and see how many deal with the theme of *heartache*. You'll likely find at least a few. And if you looked at the country music list, sister, that number would jump way up. (No offense to country music fans!)

You see, heartache's a common theme in music because it's a common theme in life. Most songs tend to deal with the boy-meets-girl, girl-loves-boy, boy-leaves-girl kind of heartache. But heartache comes in a variety of shapes and sizes. It comes when your parents split up. Or when someone you love gets sick or dies. It comes when you fail badly after you thought you'd succeed—you don't make the team or get the part or win the award. It comes when you don't get invited to the party. Or when girls at school say nasty things about you. Or when someone you trust stabs you in the back.

Whatever form it comes in—the bottom line is that it's agonizing. And though they call it heartache, a lot more than your heart hurts. You feel the pain deep in your gut, and it weighs your whole body down. And if it's bad enough, you just might feel like you're going under—so overwhelmed that you don't know if you can keep on going. But you can.

How? You cast your cares on God. Like casting a fishing line, you toss your cares out there—only you don't reel them back in. You fling them out, hurling them as far away from you as possible. Whether big or small cares, you can release them all to God. He won't let you be crushed under the weight of your heartaches.

So take your hurt and your cares to God in prayer, and learn to leave them with him. Trust in his love for you and in his power to take care of your problems. Know that he will sustain you—he'll never, ever let you fall.

 DAVID SHARED AN EXPERIENCE WHERE HE CAST HIS CARES ON GOD IN PSALM 34.

 Father, I thank you that you care about my heartache. Help me to let go of my cares and give them to you...

Drama Queen Meltdown

[Moses] asked the LORD, "Why have you brought this trouble on your servant? What have I done to displease you that you put the burden of all these people on me? I cannot carry all these people by myself; the burden is too heavy for me. If this is how you are going to treat me, put me to death right now—if I have found favor in your eyes—and do not let me face my own ruin."

Numbers 11:11,14-15

Talk about a drama queen! (In this case…king.) Moses felt completely overwhelmed with leading the people of Israel. Can't you just picture him losing it while he's talking to God? "God, why *me*?! It's too much! I can't take another day of this. At this point I'd rather die!" Yep, totally overwhelmed, losing his composure, blowing everything out of proportion.

Do you ever feel like that? Sometimes it feels as if God gives you more than you can handle: fighting with your parents, finding out your friend's pregnant, being overloaded with homework, balancing a way-too-packed schedule. It feels like way more than you can deal with. Actually, sometimes it *is* more than you can handle—at least alone.

A lot of girls try to carry their burdens on their own and wind up depressed or stressed out. Some girls funnel that stress into eating disorders (something they feel they can control) or drugs or alcohol (a false sense of escape). But God never intended you to carry your burdens by yourself.

First line of defense: God. He's available 24-7 to help carry your load.

Second line of defense: Others. Just as God provided other leaders to help Moses, so he also provides others for you to lean on—your parents, pastors, youth leaders, and Christian friends.

Before you get to the meltdown phase, make the most of the resources God has given you. He doesn't intend for you to carry the burden yourself.

 FOR THE WHOLE STORY OF MOSES' MELTDOWN AND THE HELP GOD PROVIDED, READ NUMBERS 11:4-17.

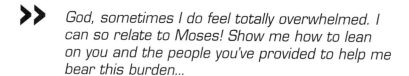 *God, sometimes I do feel totally overwhelmed. I can so relate to Moses! Show me how to lean on you and the people you've provided to help me bear this burden...*

If Only

I have learned the secret of being content in any and every situation, whether well fed or hungry, whether living in plenty or in want. I can do everything through him who gives me strength.

Philippians 4:12b-13

If only I had straight hair...if only I were 10 pounds thinner...if only that guy in my English class would notice me. If only. Sometimes our lives are ruled by the "if onlys" and the "what ifs" and the "I wishes." We blame our current unhappiness on all the things we wish were different in our lives. We're sure that if we could change those things, *then* we'd be happy or feel satisfied with life.

But have you noticed that it doesn't really work that way? Say you beg and plead for a certain pair of jeans. But then you wish you had the belt to go with them, and then the really cute purse that matches the belt, and then shoes to go with the purse. Or say you think you'll have it made when you get your driver's license. But after you get your license, you realize it's not that much fun without your own car. So you save up to buy a beater, all the while wishing you had the money to get something nicer. It's an endless cycle, isn't it? You never really arrive. You never have it all.

Paul taught that true contentment doesn't come from our circumstances. It's not based on what you have or your situation in life.

Rather it's found in knowing Jesus and trusting that he's given you *exactly* what you need and that he's got you *exactly* where he wants you today. That can be tough to accept when the "if onlys" and the "what ifs" and the "I wishes" threaten to take over. But with God's strength, you can learn to find contentment, no matter what. When you focus on Jesus and what he wants you to *do* rather than on what you wish you *had*, you will find genuine contentment.

 Check out the rest of what Paul says about contentment in Philippians 4:10-20.

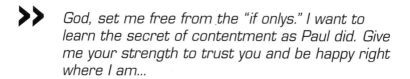 *God, set me free from the "if onlys." I want to learn the secret of contentment as Paul did. Give me your strength to trust you and be happy right where I am...*

Your Darkest Day

My soul is downcast within me. Yet this I call to mind
and therefore I have hope: Because of the Lord's great
love we are not consumed, for his compassions never fail.
They are new every morning; great is your faithfulness.

Lamentations 3:20b-23

Let's say you're feeling low. We're talking lower than low. You're so blue you couldn't possibly get any bluer. You could practically wring the tears from your pillow. You feel almost numb, and you wish you could sleep all the time. And you feel all alone—like you're the only person who's ever felt this way. Actually, though, most people experience dark places like this at some point in their lives.

Maybe that's why God included the book of Lamentations in the Bible—five chapters of Jeremiah pouring out his sorrow and pain. When you read it, you can't help but enter into the depths of his anguish. He lays it all out there: his feelings that God had abandoned him, that life's no longer worth living, and that despair and sadness are all that's left for him.

But while he's honest and real about his dark feelings, there's a ray of hope. Jeremiah chooses to hold on tight to what he knows to be true about God. He finds hope in God's character. He knows God's love and faithfulness will pull him through.

What a good model for your darkest days. When you're hurting, don't pretend that you're not. Be honest about how you feel. But recognize that your feelings aren't in charge. Remember that there's hope, there's *always* hope, for those who follow Jesus. In those darkest moments, come back to what you know to be true about God—that he's good, he's loving, he's powerful, and he's strong. He won't leave you alone in those dark moments.

 Read how Jeremiah held on to what he knew to be true of God in Lamentations 3:19-33.

 Father, my feelings tell me to give up. My feelings tell me my life is hopeless. Help me not to listen to my feelings. I want to hold on tight to you—to your love, your kindness, your mercy, your faithfulness...

Diamonds Are a Girl's Best Friend

We rejoice in the hope of the glory of God. Not only so, but we also rejoice in our sufferings, because we know that suffering produces perseverance; perseverance, character; and character, hope.

Romans 5:2b-4

Little girls love costume jewelry. Big, bright, gaudy rhinestones. Fake pearl necklaces. Sparkling, phony diamonds. At one point in your life, you probably got decked out in layer upon layer of the stuff and loved showing off your "riches." But as little girls grow up, they learn that their costume jewelry has little or no value compared to the real thing. It's just a poor, gaudy imitation of something truly precious and beautiful. (Given the choice, wouldn't any woman trade her cubic zirconium for a real diamond?)

Did you know that compared to heaven, earth is like costume jewelry? It's a pale reflection of the truly magnificent things to come. Because of what Jesus accomplished through his death on the cross, we have so much to look forward to! We have better things waiting for us—priceless treasures in glory that we can't even begin to imagine.

Unfortunately we so easily forget that. We think about life on earth as if it was the real treasure, and we're too easily satisfied with the imitation. And that's where suffering comes in handy.

What?! Yes, suffering can actually be a good thing. It reminds us that earth is not all it's cracked up to be. It helps us look forward to something better. Persevering through suffering deepens our character and reminds us to find our joy in the hope of the glory of God. And because of this, we can rejoice in our sufferings.

The next time something tough comes your way, let it serve as a reminder. Let it remind you of the incredible, genuine riches you have waiting for you in heaven. Let it remind you of all the blessings of your salvation. Keep holding out for the real thing.

 READ ROMANS 5:1-11 TO DISCOVER MORE OF THE GENUINE RICHES THAT WILL PROVIDE JOY IN ANY CIRCUMSTANCE.

 God, I confess that I tend to look for my happiness in things that don't really last. I want the tough times in my life to help me let go of the costume jewelry of earth and focus on the real treasures of heaven...

Bigger and Better

When Mary reached the place where Jesus was and saw him,
she fell at his feet and said, "Lord, if you had been here, my
brother would not have died." When Jesus saw her weeping,
and the Jews who had come along with her also weeping,
he was deeply moved in spirit and troubled.

John 11:32-33

Can you feel the pain in Mary's question? She and her sister, Martha,
and their brother, Lazarus, were tight with Jesus. When Lazarus became deathly sick, the sisters sent a message to Jesus and expected
him to come quickly to heal their brother. But Jesus didn't come, and
they watched Lazarus die. You know they must have wondered, *Jesus,
where are you? Why didn't you help us? Don't you care?*

Oh, but Jesus did care. When he arrived and saw Mary's pain,
it moved him deeply. Jesus cares intensely about your hurt, too. He
loves you, and when he sees your heart breaking, his heart breaks for
you—just the way it broke for Mary and Martha.

"Well," you might ask, "if he cares so much, why didn't he stop
this thing from happening to me? Where was he when this pain tore
my life apart?" Good questions. Remember, Mary and Martha asked
the same thing.

Before meeting up with the sisters, Jesus answered that question for his disciples in John 11:4. He said that God allowed this to happen so that he would be glorified. He had a plan in place to do even bigger and better things than Mary and Martha had imagined.

No matter how bad things get, you can trust God to work through even the most painful situations in your life for your good and for his glory—which is what life's really all about. And when God doesn't act in the way you'd hoped, at the time that you'd hoped, you can trust that he has a plan that is bigger and better than anything you could even begin to imagine.

 READ THE AMAZING STORY OF GOD'S "BIGGER AND BETTER" PLAN FOR MARY AND MARTHA (AND LAZARUS) IN JOHN 11:1-44.

 God, I know that your way is always best. Help me to know that no matter what happens in my life, you love me and care about me. Help me to trust that you're working things out in extraordinary ways...

Better Than a Frozen Java

Praise be to the God and Father of our Lord Jesus Christ, the Father of compassion and the God of all comfort, who comforts us in all our troubles, so that we can comfort those in any trouble with the comfort we ourselves have received from God.

2 Corinthians 1:3-4

Imagine this: You're at an all-time energy low, in desperate need of a refreshing frozen coffee drink. You happen to turn on your kitchen faucet, and surprise! An endless supply of the stuff comes flowing out, in any flavor you want—caramel, mocha, toffee nut, java chip. Not only are you able to satisfy your own caffeine craving, but you've also got plenty of overflow to treat all your caffeine-dependent friends. Incredible, right? And impossible, of course.

But let's translate that concept back into reality. When you're hurting and in desperate need of comfort, you can find an endless supply of that comfort in God. He's the Father of compassion and the God of all comfort. And he comforts us in all—not some, but *all*—of our troubles. God never gets tired of comforting, supporting, and consoling us. And one of the reasons he does this is so that we can pass that comfort on to others.

God wants us to take the overflow of what we receive from him and pass that on to those who are hurting. While you may never know all the reasons why God allows hard things in your life, you can see good come out of it when you put your arm around someone else and help her because you understand what she's going through.

What hard times has God brought you through? How have you found comfort in your relationship with him? How can you turn around and help others in that same situation? Don't keep God's comfort to yourself. Be ready and willing to pass it on every chance you get.

 LISTEN TO PAUL EXPLAIN HOW HE RECEIVED GOD'S COMFORT, AND THE ENCOURAGEMENT HE FOUND IN PASSING THAT ON TO OTHERS IN 2 CORINTHIANS 1:3-11.

 God, it's hard for me to understand why bad things happen in my life. Help me to trust you and turn to you for comfort. Open my eyes to see the opportunities you provide for sharing that comfort with others...

Totally Revealing

[Job's] wife said to him, "Are you still holding on to your integrity?
Curse God and die!" He replied, "You are talking like a foolish
woman. Shall we accept good from God, and not trouble?"
In all this, Job did not sin in what he said.

Job 2:9-10

Remember the last time you had a horrible, no-good, terrible, very bad day? We're talking about the kind of day that starts out bad and goes downhill from there. You sleep through your alarm and wake up to your mom yelling that you're late for school. You barely make it to class, and then you realize your shirt's inside out, and you have a huge zit on your nose. Your first class starts with a pop quiz on the chapter you forgot to read last night. That's when you realize that you just started your period. And it's not even 9 a.m. yet.

Well, Job could beat you in a "bad day" contest, no question. In a single day, invaders stole all his wealth, and a house collapsed and killed all 10 of his children. To top it off, he was then covered with painful sores from the soles of his feet to the top of his head. Talk about a really, really bad day.

But you know, hard times have a way of revealing a person's character. When hardship hit her family, Job's wife responded badly. She lost sight of God, was overwhelmed by the pain, and revealed her wimpy faith. In contrast, Job responded with integrity. He chose to trust God in the hard times just as he had in the good times. His response revealed the depth of his faith and the strength of his convictions.

What about you? When trouble comes your way, what will your response reveal about your character? Will others see in you a shallow love for God and a weak faith? Or will they see a deep love for God and a strong faith that trusts in him?

 READ MORE OF WHAT HAPPENED TO JOB AND HIS RESPONSE IN JOB 1:13-22 AND 2:7-10.

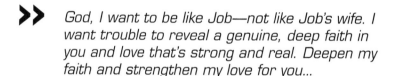 *God, I want to be like Job—not like Job's wife. I want trouble to reveal a genuine, deep faith in you and love that's strong and real. Deepen my faith and strengthen my love for you...*

Oh, Grow Up!

Consider it pure joy, my brothers, whenever you face trials of many kinds, because you know that the testing of your faith develops perseverance. Perseverance must finish its work so that you may be mature and complete, not lacking anything.

James 1:2-4

The last thing you want to be known as is *immature.* You want others to see you as the mature person you consider yourself to be, right? Well, God's tool for developing maturity may seem odd, but here it is: trials.

You see, God uses the hard things in life to help your faith "grow up." When your faith is tested, you have a choice: You can run from God and try to fix things in your own strength and in your own way; or you can keep on walking with God and doing the right things as you endure the trial. If you make the choice to persevere, then your faith grows, deepens, and matures.

Now don't misunderstand. James isn't talking about the kind of maturity that means you can decide your own curfew, watch whatever you want, and dress like your favorite pop diva. Nope. This kind of maturity means you have a grown-up faith that's complete. It means you're ready to face the challenges of life because you know where to go for help. It means you can face whatever the future holds because you've learned to hold on to God in the past.

Most of us go out of our way to avoid trials. But no matter how hard we try, they find us anyway. So when they do, stop trying to avoid them. Settle in and learn the lessons God wants to teach you. Be glad that you're on the road to maturity, even though it's hard. And remember that this maturity will carry you through both the trials of the present and the challenges of the future.

 To LEARN MORE ABOUT TRIALS AND TEMPTATIONS, READ JAMES 1:2-16.

 God, you know I'd always prefer to take the easy way out. I'm asking you to change my perspective so that I can rejoice even in the trials you bring my way. Help me to respond to hard things in such a way that my faith grows up...

God's Kind of Girl

Therefore, I tell you, her many sins have been forgiven—for she loved much. But he who has been forgiven little loves little.

Luke 7:47

Some people think that God's kind of girl is a perfect girl. You know, the girl who's never made a mistake in her life (unless you count that one math problem she missed in seventh grade), who has a perfect family, and a spotless past.

But in God's eyes, people are all the same—whether the wounds they carry from the battles of life look like amputations or light scratches. In God's eyes, each of us is nothing but a sinner. And believe it or not, a sinner is God's kind of girl. She knows how rotten her situation is without God. She's desperate for him. *That* is God's kind of girl.

Want some evidence? Then turn to Matthew 1, Jesus' family tree. You'll see a list of unpronounceable Jewish men's names with a few women's names sprinkled in. Take a look at who's on Jesus' illustrious list:

Meet Tamar—a widow who tricked her father-in-law into sleeping with her. Meet Rahab—a foreign prostitute who helped the Israelite spies. Meet Bathsheba—King David's partner in adultery.

Talk about a sketchy family line! These were women with sordid pasts. Given all the seemingly "perfect" women who have ever lived, why did God make a point to choose these women for his family tree?

To make a point. To show that God loves sinners and fixes our messed-up lives. To show that Jesus is an equal-opportunity Savior. To show that it's often those who have been forgiven the most who love God the most. To show you that God not only forgives you, but he also wants to use you in his plan. To remind you that no matter what you've gone through, no matter what you've done or what's been done to you, God considers you his kind of girl.

 Read more of Tamar's soap-opera story in Genesis 38:1-30.

 God, you know my imperfect past. Help me to let go of the pain of my past and let you make me whole. Thank you that you love me, accept me, and want to use me, just as I am...

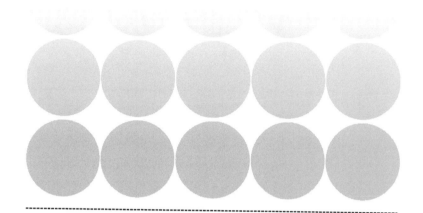

Section 5

A Style of Your Own

Way to Be Different!

But because my servant Caleb has a different spirit and follows me wholeheartedly, I will bring him into the land.

Numbers 14:24a

Do you ever find yourself in the hallway between classes, trying to walk in one direction while it feels as if the entire rest of the school is pushing in the opposite direction? It's tough to go against the flow, isn't it?

Caleb found himself going against the flow. The majority of the people complained and argued with God because they felt like God was asking them to do the impossible. But not Caleb—he had a different spirit. (And "different" here means unique, true to himself and not a follower; not "different" as in weird.) Even though everyone else was terrified of the current residents of the Promised Land, Caleb boldly said that if God wanted them to have that land (which he did), then they had nothing to fear—God would lead them to victory! Caleb wasn't afraid to have his own style and demonstrated impressive grace under pressure. He followed God with his whole heart, even though he stood alone while doing it.

What about you? Would God also say you have a different spirit?

Take this True-False quiz:

1. When your friends make fun of someone else, you're likely to either join in or just keep quiet. (True or False?)

2. You've allowed your friends to talk you into breaking at least one of your parents' rules, such as staying out after curfew, going to a party they wouldn't have allowed, using bad language, whatever. (True or False?)

3. You form your opinions of things such as clothes, movies, or music based on what your friends think is cool or not so cool. (True or False?)

If you answered "True" to any of those questions, then it's time to take a long, hard look in the mirror and ask yourself which you'd rather be: a people-pleaser or a girl with a different spirit—with her own style—that pleases God.

 SEE HOW CALEB EARNED HIS REPUTATION AS A GUY WITH A DIFFERENT SPIRIT IN NUMBERS 13:26-14:9.

 God, you know that sometimes I just want to fit in with my friends. Show me how to have my own style and a spirit that pleases you...

You Can't Please Them All

"Crucify him!" they shouted. "Why? What crime has he committed?" asked Pilate. But they shouted all the louder, "Crucify him!" Wanting to satisfy the crowd, Pilate released Barabbas to them. He had Jesus flogged, and handed him over to be crucified.

Mark 15:13-15

Wanting to satisfy the crowd...Pilate could clearly see that Jesus was being framed, that he was innocent of the charges that were brought against him. So did Pilate do the right thing and defend Jesus, even though it was hard? Nooooo. He caved in to the pressure of the crowd and his own insecurities about his shaky standing as a leader in Judea. He chose to satisfy the crowd instead of doing the right thing.

If you haven't yet discovered it, you'll soon find that God's perspective often clashes with what pleases the crowds in our culture. Most people claim there are many ways to heaven; God says there's only one. Society tells you to get back at those who hurt you; God wants you to forgive them and let him avenge the wrong. Many think you should wait to have sex until it feels right; God says to save yourself for your husband. Often you'll find it impossible to do things God's way *and* satisfy the crowd around you.

And that's when you'll have to make a choice. Make God happy or make the crowd happy. In many situations you can't have it both ways. So start thinking through how you'll make your choice. Plan ahead how you will respond. Ask yourself now: *The next time the pressure's on and the crowd's pushing me to do the wrong thing, what will I do?* Ask God for the grace to help you make the right choice.

 CHECK OUT THE WHOLE STORY OF PILATE'S CAVING IN TO THE DEMANDS OF THE CROWD IN MARK 15:1-15.

» *Jesus, Pilate handed you over to be crucified because he gave in to the crowd. Give me the strength to stand up and do the right thing—in spite of whatever pressures I'm facing...*

Worth the Risk

My lord the king, these men have acted wickedly in all they have done to Jeremiah the prophet. They have thrown him into a cistern, where he will starve to death when there is no longer any bread in the city.

Jeremiah 38:9

Check out Ebed-Melech's boldness. He really went out on a limb when he stood up for Jeremiah and saved his life. The king had given permission to the other officials to do whatever they wanted to Jeremiah. It seemed like everyone else wanted Jeremiah dead, but that didn't stop Ebed-Melech from doing the right thing. And because Ebed-Melech trusted in God and took that risk, God spared his life when Babylon conquered Jerusalem.

When you see someone being bullied or made fun of, what do you do? When you hear rumors that your classmates are planning to play a mean prank or a nasty trick on another student, how do you handle that? When you hear awful, untrue things said about someone else, killing their reputation, what do you say?

Maybe you don't do anything. Maybe you're afraid they'll turn around and come after you next. Perhaps you're afraid your own reputation will be jeopardized in the process. Or maybe you try so hard to fit in that you don't really want to stand out like that.

But think for a minute how Jeremiah must have felt sitting in that cistern. And imagine how that student being picked on must feel. If it were you, you'd want someone to help you, right? And while that should make it easier to know the right thing to do, it doesn't mean it's always easy to do it.

You may take some heat for it—but God will bless you for defending an innocent person. Be willing to do the right thing for another, even if everyone else hates you for it. And remember, it's worth the risk.

 YOU CAN FIND OUT MORE OF WHAT HAPPENED TO JEREMIAH AND EBED-MELECH WHEN YOU READ JEREMIAH 38:1-13 AND 39:15-18.

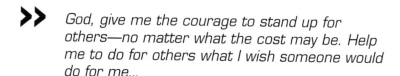 *God, give me the courage to stand up for others—no matter what the cost may be. Help me to do for others what I wish someone would do for me...*

Don't Jump!

I tell you, my friends, do not be afraid of those who kill the body and after that can do no more. But I will show you whom you should fear: Fear him who, after the killing of the body, has power to throw you into hell. Yes, I tell you, fear him.

Luke 12:4-5

If you saw a girl jump out the window of a 10-story building because she was trying to escape from a little spider, you'd think she's nuts, right? *What's she thinking?! Couldn't she see that the spider's nothing to be afraid of compared to a 10-story drop?*

That's essentially Jesus' message in Luke 12. He wanted his disciples to see how insignificant the fear of people is compared to the fear of God. You can wind up with way bigger problems if you let the fear of what others may think or do dictate your actions.

Have you ever done something stupid because you were afraid? Maybe you smoked or drank because you feared your friends would think less of you if you didn't. Maybe you slept with your boyfriend because you were afraid of losing him to another girl. Maybe you let a guy cheat off your test because you were afraid he'd make fun of you if you didn't let him.

When you care more about what other people think of you than what God thinks of you, you're headed for trouble. God's the only one we're to fear, revere, and trust. And failing to respect him is like choosing the 10-story drop over the itsy-bitsy spider. In the end, God's opinion of you is the only one that matters.

That's sometimes hard to remember, isn't it? Especially when you're getting dirty looks and your so-called friends are talking about you behind your back. But just because you can't see God doesn't make him less real than the people you fear. It's important for you to keep your relationship with God solid so that you are aware of him in your life. Then when you have to choose between the spider or the 10-story jump, you'll make the smart choice.

 CHECK OUT MORE OF JESUS' WARNINGS AND ENCOURAGEMENT ABOUT FOLLOWING GOD INSTEAD OF OTHER PEOPLE IN LUKE 12:1-12.

 God, I know I've done some stupid things because I was afraid of what others would think of me. Forgive me! Give me the courage to do what's right...

A Bold Faith

At this, the administrators and the satraps tried to find grounds for charges against Daniel in his conduct of government affairs, but they were unable to do so. They could find no corruption in him, because he was trustworthy and neither corrupt nor negligent. Finally these men said, "We will never find any basis for charges against this man Daniel unless it has something to do with the law of his God."

Daniel 6:4-5

Think of it as a political campaign. The other politicians didn't want Daniel appointed as vice-president of the kingdom, so they set out to ruin his reputation. But they ran into a little problem. They couldn't dig up a single skeleton in Daniel's closet. So they decide on a different smear tactic: they'd use his faith against him.

They had a law passed making it illegal to pray to anyone but the king. They knew Daniel would pray to his God anyway and expected that would be the end of both his political career and his life—since violating the law meant being thrown into a lion's den. Daniel had rightfully earned his reputation as a man of bold faith. His faith played a major role in how he spent his time, how he made decisions, and how he dealt with other people. He never downplayed or tried to hide his faith. And this new law didn't change any of that.

Would you share that same reputation as a person of faith? Can the people around you clearly see that your relationship with God affects your time, your choices, and your relationships? Or do you try to downplay your faith? Are you worried that people will think you're a fanatic? Do you shy away from anything that would make it obvious you're a Christian?

God used Daniel as a witness to an entire nation because he stood firm in boldly living out his faith. And God wants to use you in the same way. Live out your relationship with God—live a bold and spicy life—and you'll see God use you in incredible ways.

 SEE HOW GOD USED DANIEL'S FAITHFULNESS TO MAKE A DIFFERENCE IN DANIEL 6:1-28.

 God, sometimes it's easier not to have to deal with the flack I get over being a Christian. Change my heart and help me live boldly for you in front of my friends...

Enough Excuses!

When God nudges you to do something, do you answer the way Gideon did? *"But Lord*...I don't know enough Bible verses to tell my friends about Jesus. *But Lord*...I'm not smart enough to talk about my beliefs in science class. *But Lord*...I'm not enough of a leader to start a Bible study at school." Like Gideon, do you focus more on yourself and your weaknesses than on God and his strength?

You need to know that God's not at all fazed by your excuses. He knows what you're capable of, and if he didn't think you could do it, then he would have asked someone else! And the bottom line is that it doesn't really matter what you can or can't do—all that matters is that God will be with you, and *he* can do *all* things. You've just got to trust in him and step out in faith.

Where in your life have you been making excuses? It's time to stop saying, "But Lord, I can't" and start saying, "But Lord, I know *you* can." Share the gospel with an unsaved friend, stand up for your beliefs in class, start that Bible study. Whatever you've been holding back because you feel weak, get going on. Because God is strong! If he's called you to do something, he'll give you all the resources you need to make it happen.

 SEE HOW GOD DEMONSTRATED HIS STRENGTH THROUGH GIDEON'S WEAKNESS IN JUDGES 7:1-22.

» *God of all strength, you know I tend to focus on my weaknesses. I forget that you're not interested in what I can't do, because you can do all things through me. Show me what you want me to do, and give me the courage to do it...*

On the Hot Seat

Now, Lord, consider their threats and enable your servants to speak your word with great boldness.

Acts 4:29

When the going got tough, these believers got...bolder?! Their lives were threatened, so naturally they prayed. But do you notice what they *didn't* pray for? They *didn't* ask God to miraculously intervene and change their enemies' hearts. They *didn't* pray for God to make their lives easier and more comfortable. Instead they asked God for great boldness so they could continue to speak out in spite of any danger.

When you're on the hot seat for your faith, what are you praying for? When your teacher says the Bible is just a good work of fiction, do you pray for the boldness to challenge that opinion based on what you've learned? When people at school think it's narrow-minded and arrogant to believe there's only one way to God, do you ask God to give you the words to tell them what you believe? When your youth group leader asks you to share with the group how you became a Christ-follower, do you pray for the courage to speak?

Earlier in Acts 4, Luke (the writer of Acts) tells us that the leaders who threatened Peter and John were astonished at their courage in sharing the gospel—because these guys were ordinary, unschooled men. Their boldness to speak out about Jesus didn't come from their own natural abilities and skills. It came from their conviction that the message should be shared no matter what the cost—and they depended on God to give them the boldness and courage to do just that.

You might feel like you don't have what it takes to stand up and speak out. But it doesn't matter. God can give you the words you need and the courage to share them. Ask him to enable you to speak his word with great boldness. And go for it!

 READ THE WHOLE EXCITING STORY OF PETER AND JOHN'S BOLD WITNESS, THE THREATS THEY RECEIVED, AND THE SUBSEQUENT PRAYER OF THE BELIEVERS FOR BOLDNESS IN ACTS 4:1-31.

 God, you gave boldness to the believers in Acts, and I believe you can give me that same boldness. Help me to choose to stand up for you with that same courage, no matter how afraid I might feel...

Public Humiliation

Do you wonder what would possibly make someone volunteer for reality TV shows? Inevitably it seems that the people wind up humiliating themselves in front of an audience of thousands—sometimes millions. Their flaws, failures, and quirks are broadcast on national television for all to see. What would ever make somebody agree to go through that kind of disgrace?

Most of the participants would probably say that the humiliation was worth it. Either they won the contests and earned the prize, or they gained fame and recognition, or they had a once-in-a-lifetime experience. Most would say that any disgrace they suffered was worth it because of what they received in the process.

For the apostles, their disgrace wasn't part of a fake TV show. It was real-life all the way. And the disgrace they suffered came in the form of severe, bloody beatings. Yet they walked out of there rejoicing! Were these guys award-winning actors, or did they take some morbid delight in getting whipped? Actually they realized that suffering for Jesus was a great honor. He chose *them* to represent him before the skeptics, and that was an amazing privilege. They knew anything they suffered was more than worth the cost.

When you get laughed at or treated unfairly because of your faith, consider the fact that Jesus chose you to represent him, and that's worth celebrating. He counted *you* worthy of his name.

 SEE MORE OF THE APOSTLES' STORY AND HOW THEY REJOICED IN THE PRIVILEGE OF REPRESENTING JESUS IN ACTS 5:12-42.

>> *God, it seems a little strange to rejoice in suffering disgrace because of my faith in you. But remind me that the joy comes from knowing you're worth it, and you consider me worthy to share your name...*

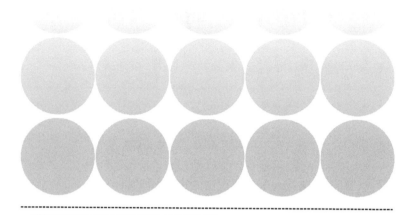

Section 6

The Most Valuable Things

Your MVP (Most Valued Possession)

> Some time later God tested Abraham. He said to him, "Abraham!" "Here I am," he replied. Then God said, "Take your son, your only son, Isaac, whom you love, and go to the region of Moriah. Sacrifice him there as a burnt offering on one of the mountains I will tell you about."
>
> Genesis 22:1-2

What do you value more than anything else? Something you own? Your reputation? Your family? Your friends? A dream for your future? Abraham loved Isaac deeply. He had waited for years for God to give him a son. So how could he even consider sacrificing him? He could do it because, more than anything else, he valued his relationship with God.

It's hard to think of losing the things you value most. Maybe you know someone whose house burned to the ground. While you feel bad for that person, you're glad it wasn't you—you'd be so bummed about losing your stuff that way! Maybe missionaries visit your church and tell stories of living without things like hot showers and their favorite breakfast cereal. You think it's great they can do that—but you know there's absolutely no way you'd be able to live like that.

Every day we have a choice: hold tightly to things and stuff we feel is important or let go and trust God to give and be for us everything we need. If God called you to let go of what earthly thing you value most, could you? If you knew that nothing on earth could compare to the treasure of God himself, then you could do it. If you believed that God would bring good things from your sacrifice, then you could do it.

When you value God above all else, then you can hold on loosely to the lesser stuff in your life. Put God first in your heart and your life and let everything else go.

 READ ABOUT ABRAHAM'S CALL TO SACRIFICE—AND THE BLESSINGS HE RECEIVED FOR ANSWERING THAT CALL—IN GENESIS 22:1-19.

 God, I know I hold on tightly to so many things besides you. I want to be willing to give up everything except for you. Help me to value you more than anyone or anything else in my life...

Sure-Fire Investing

Do not store up for yourselves treasures on earth, where moth and rust destroy, and where thieves break in and steal. But store up for yourselves treasures in heaven, where moth and rust do not destroy, and where thieves do not break in and steal. For where your treasure is, there your heart will be also.

Matthew 6:19-21

"Cute shirt. Designer?"

"Great cell. Can it take pictures, too?"

"Cool car. Is it yours or your parents'?"

It's so easy to be defined by your possessions, isn't it? You gain a certain level of respect and popularity from people when you have nice things—and lots of them. But your life is meant to be about so much more than your stuff. *You* are meant to be about so much more than your stuff.

Clothes, cell phones, cars—no matter how great these things are, they won't last forever. Clothes go out of style, cell phones break, and cars fall apart. That's why it's important to value the things you can't see—such as faith, love, and obedience to God—because they last forever.

You know, we often envy the rich and famous and imagine life would be better if we had what they have. But it's also common to "have it all" yet have nothing of any lasting value. Without Christ, life is ultimately empty. With him, you have all the riches of heaven.

So don't focus on material things. Focus on all that you have in Christ. Remember that you're worth more than the "sum of your stuff." Find ways to invest your time, money, and energy into things that will last for eternity. Now that's sure-fire investing! Spend time building your relationship with God. Reach out to someone new at school. Share the gospel with your friends. Volunteer at a soup kitchen. Donate to your church missions fund. Spend less time focusing on the temporary treasures you have on earth and more time storing up for yourself eternal treasures in heaven.

 Check out more of what Jesus had to say about focusing on the eternal instead of the temporary in Matthew 6:19-34.

 God, thank you for giving me eternal riches in you. Help me not to focus on my earthly "treasures." Show me how to invest in treasures that will last forever...

No Regrets

> What good is it for a man to gain the
> whole world, yet forfeit his soul?
>
> Mark 8:36

Picture yourself at the end of your life. Say you're a millionaire, married to a handsome actor, with celebrities as your friends and three successful children. Was it a good life? No regrets? Only if you'd spent it walking with Jesus, willing to make whatever sacrifice he asked you to make in order to love and obey him. And if you had—then that was a sweet life! But if you hadn't—there's a good chance you've gained the world but forfeited your soul.

What does that mean? It means that some people think they have it all. They amass tons of stuff: cars, houses, toys, yachts. They define "success" in shallow terms: how rich, how smart, how pretty, how famous they are. They make sure they look like "good people": they go to church, do some good deeds, make sure they're "better" than other people. But when they die, if they didn't know Jesus, then they've got *nothing*. By investing in all the wrong things, they've forfeited their souls.

Soon you'll begin making important decisions about your future: whether or not to go to college, what to do after school, what kind of career to pursue and possibly who to marry. What factors will affect your decisions? Will money, status, and comfort be the motives for your choices? Will you take the job that you think God wants you in or choose a career just because it'll earn more money? Will you marry the man you love, even if he wants to be a pastor or a missionary, or the man who can only offer you a hefty trust fund?

If you're not wise, you could build a life that gains you the whole world but costs you your soul. As you make goals for your future and choices for today, remember what's really important. Submit your hopes, your dreams, and your plans for the future to Jesus. If you do that, you'll be able to look back on your life with no regrets.

 CHECK OUT MARK 8:27-38, WHERE JESUS TALKS TO HIS DISCIPLES ABOUT CHOOSING TO FOLLOW HIM.

 God, I want to follow you with all my heart. Help me to be willing to give up whatever it takes to do that...

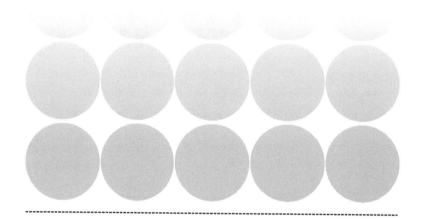

Section 7

The Relationship Factor

Shake It Up, Baby!

Dear friends, since God so loved us,
we also ought to love one another.

1 John 4:11

You know what happens when you shake a can of soda really, really hard and then open it quickly—the soda sprays all over the person holding the can and usually covers the people nearby, too. Did you know that God wants you to be like that can? God wants your life to be so full of love that it overflows and covers everyone around you.

How can a girl go about "shakin' it up" that way? You can start by focusing on God's love for you. Most girls appreciate a good love story—one filled with drama and sacrifice and passion. (Think now about your favorite dramatic movie.) Well, the Bible contains the most powerful love story ever written—the Creator of the universe dying in our place, for our sin, because he loves us so deeply. When you totally engross yourself in *the* great drama of the ages, your mind and heart will be so filled up with his love that it will overflow. And that's when you'll begin to love others the way God wants you to. Whether you feel like it or not. When it's easy, and when it's hard. Because loving others isn't optional for us—God makes it mandatory.

That kind of love is impossible on your own. It's impossible to love your enemy—that girl who tries to ruin your life. It's impossible

to love your pesky little brother all the time—especial
vades your privacy and embarrasses you in front of you
if you first let God fill you with his love, then that impo
love just became possible. So go ahead—shake it up and cover those
around you!

READ MORE OF HOW GOD'S LOVE FOR US SHOULD RESULT IN OUR
LOVING OTHERS IN 1 JOHN 4:7-21.

Jesus, thank you for loving me so much that you died for me. Your love is so incredible! Fill me up with your love so that I can cover others with your love, too...

Just Accept 'Em

At school you might expect certain people to judge you. It probably doesn't surprise you when some girls backstab and gossip about each other. Maybe you figure it's normal for different groups to have some conflict. You probably expect that kind of thing at school. But you might not expect it at church.

However, the church, like your school, is filled with sinners. That means that you can expect to deal with the same kinds of issues at church. But you can also bank on the fact that God expects better things from his children. He wants us to be different. He wants the church to demonstrate a unity that's only possible because he's at work within us.

That kind of unity begins with accepting others the same way God accepts you. You didn't have to change your personality, clothes, or interests for God to accept you. You didn't have to pretend to be someone you're not. God loves you just the way you are. And when you love others the way God loves you, that builds unity.

So when someone in your youth group makes a snide comment about you, surprise that person by overlooking that sin and accepting her despite her faults. When two girls start tearing each other down, find ways to foster peace and unity between them. (You can start by cutting off their gossip, then changing the subject, then just flat-out telling them that you'd love to see them get over this petty issue.) When you feel tension between the different subgroups in your youth group (such as the home-school, Christian school, and public school crowds), remember that God made every single student uniquely in his image. Learn to accept and appreciate those differences, and you'll become an agent for unity. And that pleases God.

 YOU'LL FIND MORE OF PAUL'S ENCOURAGEMENT TO BUILD UNITY WHEN YOU READ ROMANS 15:1-13.

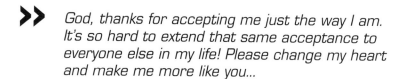 *God, thanks for accepting me just the way I am. It's so hard to extend that same acceptance to everyone else in my life! Please change my heart and make me more like you...*

It's Your Serve

So [Jesus] got up from the meal, took off his outer clothing, and wrapped a towel around his waist. After that, he poured water into a basin and began to wash his disciples' feet, drying them with the towel that was wrapped around him.

John 13:4-5

So was foot washing some kind of Jewish party game? Ummmmm, *no.* In that culture of dusty roads and sandaled feet, a servant usually had the gross, dirty job of washing the guests' feet when they arrived. So you can imagine the disciples' shock and amazement when Jesus—their teacher and leader—lowered himself to perform this menial task. Jesus did it to communicate an important message to them and to us: If he, the Son of God, could serve like that, then surely none of us is too good to serve others in whatever ways we can.

Maybe you can already think of a way that God's been prompting you to serve, but you just haven't done it yet. Time to get going! Don't put it off any longer. You'll discover that serving others is one of the most rewarding things you can do.

Maybe you're willing to serve, but you have no clue where to start. Pick something from the following list to get you going:

1. What chore does your brother or sister hate? Give your sibling a break, and do it as a surprise.

2. Know someone at school without any friends? Invite that person to join you and your friends for lunch.

3. Know a single mom? Help her out by cleaning her house or babysitting—*for free*!

4. What needs do you see in your community? Try volunteering at a local soup kitchen, crisis pregnancy center, or children's hospital.

5. Know any elderly people? Offer to do free yard work or run errands for them.

Jesus had every right to expect to be served, but instead he came to serve others. And he tells us to do the same. So wrap that towel around your waist and get moving!

 READ THE WHOLE "SHOCKING" STORY OF JESUS' SERVICE IN JOHN 13:2-17.

 God, it's easy to want people to do things for me. Change my heart. Make me like Jesus. Open my eyes to see the ways you want me to serve others...

Won't You Be My Neighbor?

But love your enemies, do good to them, and lend to them without expecting to get anything back. Then your reward will be great.

Luke 6:35a

Here's the scene: A Jewish leader wanted to trick Jesus into incriminating himself. Having established that the way to eternal life is to love God and love your neighbor, the leader asked Jesus, "So, who's my neighbor?" Jesus responded with the well-known parable of the Good Samaritan.

Now if Jesus told the parable to us today, he just might tell it this way:

A clean-cut, straight-A student was walking through a rough neighborhood when a gang beat her up, robbed her, and left her for dead.

A member of the girl's youth group happened to be walking through the same neighborhood. But he was late for a meeting and nervous about the area, and he thought he probably couldn't do much anyway...so he walked by.

Then along came the student body president from her school, on his way to volunteer at the local soup kitchen (which he thought would look great on his college applications). [ ] way, pretending not to see her.

Another guy from her school also happened [ ] of town. This guy was sketchy—he dressed weird a [ ] like he was smoking something. The injured girl never would have condescended to talk to this guy. But he stopped to help her. He called an ambulance, stayed with her at the hospital, and brought her flowers. He was the one—not the others—who loved his neighbor.

You see, what made the "good Samaritan" so good was that he went out of his way to help someone who would have viewed him as an enemy or an inferior—and who probably never would have helped him.

So how can you go out of your way to love someone who isn't expecting it? Do you have a rival or know someone who's always mean to you? Loving your neighbor means looking for opportunities to love even that person—*especially* that person.

 READ THE ENTIRE STORY THE WAY JESUS TOLD IT IN
LUKE 10:25-37.

 God, don't let me be like those who ignored the person in need. Give me opportunities to show mercy, even to my enemies, and help me to truly love my neighbor...

Pass the Peace, Please

Therefore, if you are offering your gift at the altar and there remember that your brother has something against you, leave your gift there in front of the altar. First go and be reconciled to your brother; then come and offer your gift.

Matthew 5:23-24

Say you got in a fight with your mom, your sister, or a friend. You think, *It happens to everybody. I'm just gonna ride it out. We both said some things we didn't mean, but we'll get over it. No need to make a big deal out of it, right?* Nope, no way, nuh-uh. That's just not God's way. To him, conflict is a big deal.

If you've got issues with somebody, then God wants you to deal with them. He wants you to be a peacemaker. That means he wants you to promote the peace and unity that's part of who he is. Yeah, maybe everybody else thinks it's fine to ignore the issue—but not God. He wants us to approach conflict his way.

Of course you'll disagree about certain things with other people. Of course there will be things you won't see eye-to-eye on with everybody else. But how you handle those things is crucial. If you can keep it from escalating into a fight in the first place, that's definitely God's "Plan A." Work hard to find ways to work out your differences.

But if you're past that point already, then move on to "Plan B" and do everything you can to make it right. It's so important to God that he wants you to straighten things out with other people before you come to him. (Which doesn't mean you should put off coming to God—it means you should get in gear and go make things right!) Don't ignore the problem and hope it will go away. That kind of stuff never really goes away; it just festers under the surface. As much as you might want to ignore or run from it, you've just got to deal with it.

 SEE MORE OF WHAT JESUS SAID ABOUT THE THINGS THAT PROMOTE PEACE IN MATTHEW 5:3-10, 21-26.

 God, I know that you're a God of peace. Help me to do whatever it takes to bring your peace to my relationships...

Upping the Ante

Then Peter came to Jesus and asked, "Lord, how many times shall I forgive my brother when he sins against me? Up to seven times?" Jesus answered, "I tell you, not seven times, but seventy-seven times."

Matthew 18:21-22

Leave it to Peter. Suggesting you should forgive someone not just once, not even twice, but *seven* times. He thought he was really being generous. But then Jesus ups the ante—and tells Peter to forgive *77* times. And Jesus doesn't mean you should literally keep a running tally. He's saying there should be no limit on forgiveness.

Jesus illustrates this with the story of a king who forgives an outrageously large debt (like millions of dollars) that his servant owes him. That servant then refuses to forgive a much smaller debt (like 10 measly bucks) that a fellow servant owes him. The king has the first servant punished for failing to show the other servant the same mercy the king had shown him. Ouch!

In other words, Jesus is saying it's ludicrous to withhold forgiveness from others when God has forgiven you for so much. As long as others keep on sinning against you, that's how long you keep forgiving them. Because that's what God does with you.

You might feel like that person doesn't deserve forgiveness—but remember, neither do you. You might worry that you're letting the person off easy—but remember that justice belongs to God, in his way and in his time. You might feel as though forgiving someone means that what that person did to you was okay; but don't forget that forgiveness means you trust God to use all things—even the hurt others inflict on you—for your good and his glory.

When someone gossips about you, shamelessly flirts with your boyfriend, betrays you, forgets your birthday, makes fun of you, or hurts you deeply...forgive that person because God has forgiven you. And if that person does it again (and again and again!), you have to keep on forgiving—because God keeps on forgiving you.

 READ MATTHEW 18:21-35 FOR THE FULL STORY OF THE INDEBTED SERVANT.

 God, remind me how great your mercy has been in forgiving my sin. Help me to keep that in perspective so I can forgive others each and every time they sin against me...

Mean Girls

Do not repay anyone evil for evil. Be careful to do what is right in the eyes of everybody. If it is possible, as far as it depends on you, live at peace with everyone. Do not take revenge, my friends, but leave room for God's wrath, for it is written: "It is mine to avenge; I will repay," says the Lord.

Romans 12:17-19

Every school has them. You'll even find them in many churches. Who are they? They're the *mean girls*. They think they own the place. They've found a way to wield power, and they can be nasty about it. If you do things their way, you might be safe. But dare to cross them, and you're in for it.

The temptation, when facing a mean girl, is to fight fire with fire. To find a way to get back or to get even. And while such tactics may be temporarily satisfying, they sure don't honor God. Instead of ridding the world of one mean girl, all you do is add another to the list...*you!*

So what should you do instead? Do everything in your power to be at peace, and trust that God will deal with the mean girl in his own way. Do what's right—respond with grace and kindness, no matter how hard it is. Paul says in Romans 12:21, "Do not be overcome by evil, but overcome evil with good."

Take the high road. Don't lower yourself to using the mean girl's tactics against her. Show mercy and love instead. You might be surprised. The meanest girls are often the ones who've been hurt the most themselves. They work hard to come across so strong because on the inside they're completely insecure.

If you've got someone like that in your life right now, sit down and make a list of the practical ways you can meet that person's attacks with a defense of compassion, patience, gentleness, and love. And ask God for the strength to repay evil with good.

 READ ROMANS 12:9-21 FOR MORE PRACTICAL ADVICE ON LOVING THE DIFFICULT PEOPLE IN YOUR LIFE.

 Lord, help me see others through your eyes. Help me see even the meanest person as someone in need of mercy and compassion. Show me how to love like you love...

A Soap Opera Story

When they kept on questioning him, he straightened up
and said to them, "If any one of you is without sin, let
him be the first to throw a stone at her."

John 8:7

What a soap opera plot: A woman is caught in the act of adultery.
Yanked from her bed and hauled out, probably half-clothed, into the
temple courts. But her accusers don't really care about her and her
sin. What they really want is to use the situation to trap Jesus. Their
hatred for Jesus runs so deep that they're willing to destroy this poor
woman in order to stain Jesus' reputation.

And then the plot twist no one anticipated—Jesus, who knows
their hearts, turns the whole thing back on the accusers. Instead of
letting them make the issue about the woman and her sin, he makes
it about them and their sin. One by one, they all turn away. Not a
single one throws a stone.

It's easy to read that story and come down hard on the woman's
accusers. But first stop and take a look at yourself. Are you also quick
to point out and condemn others for their sins—all while forgetting
that you're guilty, too? Nobody's perfect and that includes you. Girl,
you've got to remember that we all have issues. Some of our sin is

really public. Other sin we hide and guard closely so no one else knows about it. But either way, God sees it.

Now if anyone had a right to condemn the woman caught in adultery, it was Jesus, the righteous Judge. He alone could have cast that stone. But he didn't. Although he didn't condone her sin (you'll have to check out the end of the story), instead of throwing stones, he offered her compassion. It's time for you to do the same. Put down your rock and extend to others the same mercy that you would want them to show you if your sins were exposed.

 READ THE WHOLE "SOAP OPERA" FOR YOURSELF IN JOHN 8:1-11.

 Jesus, thank you for being a compassionate Judge. Remind me of the mercy you've shown me so that I'll be quick to extend that same mercy and grace to others...

Section 8

Friendship 101

Don't Be a Loner

Two are better than one, because they have a good return for their work: If one falls down, his friend can help him up. But pity the man who falls and has no one to help him up!

Ecclesiastes 4:9-10

Two really are better than one. Sometimes it's hard to believe this—especially when you've been hurt by a close friend and feel like you don't want to let anyone too close to you for a while. But God didn't design us to go through life on our own. A good friend can pick you up when you fall and make everything seem better just because she's with you.

Do you want a friend like that? Then start by *being* a friend like that. Good friendships don't just happen; you have to invest in them. You have to choose to be vulnerable and to think about someone else first. And sometimes you do get hurt in the process. Building and growing good friendships takes a lot of time and effort—but it's *so* worth it! In a truly great friendship, you both feel like you receive even more than you give, and you know it's worth every bit of the work.

Find in the Bible where it's written that a girl can only have one "best friend"! (You won't find it, by the way.) In fact, in Ecclesiastes 4:12 Solomon writes, "a cord of three strands is not quickly broken." Some girls latch on to a single best friend and close themselves off from anyone else. But there's plenty of room in your heart and life for more than just one friend. There's so much to be gained from having a variety of close friends. When you invest in friendships, you'll find that the return on your investment is priceless.

 SEE WHAT SOLOMON SAYS ABOUT THE VALUE OF FRIENDSHIP IN ECCLESIASTES 4:7-12.

>> *God, sometimes my friends are a pain, but I know they're a gift from you. Help me to invest myself in my friends and to be a good friend to them...*

The Model Friendship

Jonathan became one in spirit with David, and he loved him as himself. And Jonathan made a covenant with David because he loved him as himself.

1 Samuel 18:1b, 3

Do you have a bosom buddy, a real kindred spirit? Jonathan and David had that kind of friendship. Their relationship was an amazing model of the kind of friendships God wants us to pursue.

In what ways? Well, they were willing to do anything for each other. They had a "what's mine is yours" attitude. They helped each other look at life from God's perspective. They made promises to each other—and sacrificed a great deal to keep them. They focused on what they could give to their friendship, not on what they could get from it. For example, Jonathan was the crowned prince, yet he did everything he could to help his best friend David become the next king. Talk about selfless!

You probably already know that this kind of friendship requires you to give a lot of yourself. You should also know that you won't develop this with every girlfriend you have. In fact, this friendship requires you to be selective. Because when you become so close with another that you're "one in spirit," as Jonathan and David were, then you start to become like each other. You may begin to use the same phrases, develop the same mannerisms, even dress alike. More importantly, your attitudes about God and what's important in life rub off on each other. So pick your closest friends wisely. While it's healthy to be friends with all kinds of girls—and to make sure you have some non-Christian friends as well—your absolute closest friend should be a Christian, a girl who wants to grow spiritually, so that you two can encourage each other.

David and Jonathan had the rare kind of friendship we all long for. If God gives you a friendship like that, be thankful! And if you don't have this yet, continue to be a good friend to others and patiently wait for God to develop that friendship for you.

 READ 1 SAMUEL 20:1-42 FOR AN EXAMPLE OF HOW DAVID AND JONATHAN EXPRESSED THEIR FRIENDSHIP TO EACH OTHER.

 God, I want the kind of friendship that David and Jonathan had. Help me to look for good friends and to be a good friend...

Friendship for Dummies

Clothe yourselves with compassion, kindness, humility, gentleness and patience. Bear with each other and forgive whatever grievances you may have against one another. Forgive as the Lord forgave you. And over all these virtues put on love, which binds them all together in perfect unity.

Colossians 3:12b-14

Anne of Green Gables has Diana. SpongeBob has Patrick. Luke Skywalker has Hans Solo. Frodo has Sam. And the Three Musketeers all have each other. But maybe *you* feel as if you have no one. Maybe you have acquaintances, even casual friends, but you don't have a true-blue, stick-to-you-like-glue kind of friend.

It's not that you don't want a friend like that. You do! But making friends can be tough—especially when you move to a new place or start going to a new school or new church. In those situations making any friends can seem hard—and making deep, lasting friendships can seem downright impossible!

But God gives you a starting place: Begin by being a good friend to those around you. How? Check out the Bible—it's God's "Relationship How-To Guide." (You could call it the ultimate *Friendship for Dummies* manual.) The Bible's filled with God's guidelines for how you should treat others. Did you catch a few of those tips from the verses in Colossians? Treat others with compassion, kindness, humility, gentleness, and patience. Be quick to forgive. Let love be the driving force behind all your actions. Wouldn't you want to be friends with someone who does all that?

So if you're on the hunt for some quality friends, focus less on your lack of friends and more on reaching out and being a friend to others. Dig into God's Word for more practical tips. As you apply what you read, you'll begin to develop relationships. And over time, God may deepen at least one of those relationships to give you a Diana, or a Patrick, or a Sam...or even a Musketeer!

 PAUL WANTS US TO FOCUS OUR HEARTS ON CHRIST AND THEN ON OTHERS. READ MORE OF HOW HE SAYS TO DO THIS IN COLOSSIANS 3:1-17.

 God, you know how badly I want a real, true friend. Thank you that you are that kind of friend. Help me to be that kind of friend to others and to wait on you to deepen my relationships...

Loyal to the End

But Ruth replied, "Don't urge me to leave you or to turn back from you. Where you go I will go, and where you stay I will stay. Your people will be my people and your God my God. Where you die I will die, and there I will be buried. May the Lord deal with me, be it ever so severely, if anything but death separates you and me."

Ruth 1:16-17

Ever had a friend dump you at the first sign of trouble? That's not loyalty. It's those tough times when you need a friend the most! You should be able to count on your true friends even when you're having a major PMS day, when you're not feeling lively or fun, when you're going through an ugly stage, when you just can't get your act together. A true friend loves at *all* times—through the good *and* the bad.

That's what Ruth did. You could call her the poster-girl for loyalty. She left her friends, her family, her home, and all that was familiar to support her grieving mother-in-law, Naomi—knowing that Naomi couldn't give her anything in return. She knew that loving Naomi was the right thing to do, and she committed herself to Naomi to the very end. Ruth's choice reflected God's work in her life.

And though Ruth gave up a great deal out of love and loyalty to Naomi, God repaid her with amazing blessings. Her sacrifice did not go unnoticed by a certain amazing, godly, wealthy, very-eligible bachelor named Boaz, either. And the rest, as they say, is history.

While you may not win the man of your dreams as a reward for your loyalty to your friends, you can trust that God will bless you for it. God's always faithful to us, never leaves us, and always loves us. When we love the people he's put in our lives in the same way, he also repays whatever sacrifices we make with amazing blessings.

 FOR RUTH'S WHOLE DRAMATIC STORY, READ RUTH 1. (IF YOU WANT TO SEE HOW THE LOVE STORY PLAYS OUT, READ THE REST OF RUTH—IT'S ONLY THREE MORE CHAPTERS!)

 God, thanks for being with me through both the good and the bad in my life. Help me to show the same loyalty to the people in my life...

Say What?!

Do not let any unwholesome talk come out of your mouths,
but only what is helpful for building others up according
to their needs, that it may benefit those who listen.

Ephesians 4:29

If all the words you said last week were written down, would they show that you didn't let *any* unwholesome talk come out of your mouth, but *only* what builds others up? That's a pretty tough command to keep—especially when you're with your friends. Though it's hard, you've still got to do your best to obey. Makes you want to yell for help, doesn't it?

Well, if the apostle Paul wrote an advice column—like Dear Abby or Dr. Laura—on how to use your words when you're with your friends, it might read something like this:

Today's column features Dr. Paul's handy-dandy list of do's and don'ts for talking to your friends:

- *Do* speak the truth. Be honest and real.

- *Don't* deceive others and pretend to be something or someone you're not.

- *Do* get rid of slander. As the saying goes, "If you can't say something nice, don't say anything at all."

- *Don't* use obscenity, foolish talk, or coarse jokes. If you're not sure what that means, follow this rule of thumb: If you can't say it to your pastor, you probably shouldn't say it to your friends.

- *Do* speak to each other about the stuff that really matters. Talk about God and the good things he's done in your life.

- *Don't* let unwholesome words come out of your mouth. Never tear others down, even in "fun." Saying "she knows I'm only kidding" doesn't make it any less hurtful. Resist the temptation to make yourself look better by pointing out someone else's faults.

- *Do* say things that will build others up and benefit those who listen to you. Go out of your way to say encouraging things about others and to others.

Rely on God for the strength to use the power of your words to make a positive difference in the lives of your friends!

 CHECK OUT MORE OF "DR. PAUL'S ADVICE" ON BOTH YOUR ACTIONS AND WORDS IN EPHESIANS 4:22-5:20.

 God, I want to pay more attention to my words. Help me use my words to help others instead of hurt them...

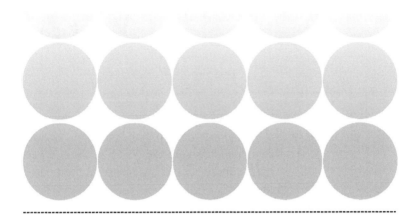

Section 9

The Guy/Girl Riddle

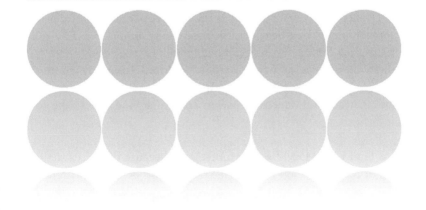

Want Ad

But the Lᴏʀᴅ said to Samuel, "Do not consider his appearance
or his height, for I have rejected him. The Lᴏʀᴅ does not look
at the things man looks at. Man looks at the outward
appearance, but the Lᴏʀᴅ looks at the heart."

1 Samuel 16:7

If you wrote a "want ad" for the perfect guy, what would it say?
*Wanted: Boyfriend. Must be tall (at least 5'11"), with amazing eyes
(preferably blue), and a fabulous smile. Any hair color acceptable, but no
shaved heads, please. Broad shoulders and well-defined arms, a definite
plus.* If we're honest, most of us will admit that we're drawn to good-
looking guys. But have you noticed how a really handsome guy can
suddenly become way less attractive if he's a total jerk?

When God was choosing a king to replace Saul, he told the
prophet Samuel that he'd find the future king among the eight sons
of Jesse. But Samuel wasn't supposed to look for the handsomest, the
tallest, the strongest, or the smartest. God told Samuel to ignore all
the external things, even though most people get hung up on that
stuff. Instead God wanted Samuel to value what God valued: the new
king's heart.

God chose David as the future king because of the attractive-
ness of his heart. God knew that David would be a man who loved

God deeply, who cared about the things God cared about, who made mistakes but still followed hard after God. And *that's* the kind of guy God was looking for.

Is that the kind of guy *you're* looking for? Let's think about re-writing that "want ad." Maybe something more along the lines of this: *Wanted: Guy who's totally committed to God. Whose love for God produces a real love for others. Must be patient, generous, and quick to forgive. Humble and teachable spirit preferred. Strong convictions a definite plus.*

 Find out more about Samuel's search for the perfect guy when you read 1 Samuel 16:1-13.

 God, help me to look beyond appearances to the heart. Help me to look for a guy who puts you first in his heart and life...

Worth the Wait

Now Naomi had a relative on her husband's side...a man
of standing, whose name was Boaz. As it turned out,
[Ruth] found herself working in a field belonging to Boaz.

Ruth 2:1,3b

Going stag. Flying solo. Table for one. Yep, that's you. You've basically resigned yourself to spending all your Friday nights alone from now until eternity.

Ruth probably figured she'd be single forever, too. Ruth was a young widow and a foreigner in an unfamiliar land. Men in Israel didn't think much of girls from Moab. Ruth's chances of ever getting married again, especially to a quality guy, were next to zero.

So did Ruth sit around binging on chocolate and moaning to her mother-in-law about her miserable situation? No way! She kept living. She looked at how she could serve God and take care of her mother-in-law. She worked hard—without concern for herself. Little did she know that all the while God was preparing her to meet the man of her dreams.

Enter Boaz—a "man of standing," meaning people respected him. He followed God's law wholeheartedly at a time when most people disregarded it almost completely. Boaz was humble, kind, and gentle. He worked hard and became wealthy. And he was incredibly smart. Yeah, Boaz was definitely at the top of Bethlehem's "most eligible bachelor" list. The Bible doesn't tell us why Boaz hadn't married earlier. But it seems likely he'd been waiting for God to bring the right girl—a godly girl—into his life.

Enter Ruth. She quickly caught Boaz's attention. He saw her love for God and her loyalty and devotion to Naomi—and he was impressed.

Find hope in Ruth's story. Just because you're single now doesn't mean you'll be single forever. And the right guy is worth the wait. While you wait, make the most of your time. Stay focused on your relationship with Jesus. Get involved in serving others. At the right time, if it's his plan for you to be married, God will surprise you both with the gift of each other.

 READ THE STORY OF RUTH AND BOAZ'S FIRST MEETING IN RUTH 2:1-18.

 God, it's hard when all my friends have guys in their lives. Help me to wait for you to bring the right guy at the right time. Keep my eyes focused on growing in you while I wait...

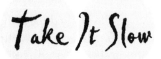

Take It Slow

Do not arouse or awaken love until it so desires.

Song of Songs 2:7b

Do not arouse or awaken love until it so desires. What does *that* mean? It means let love develop naturally. It means don't force it, don't manipulate circumstances to speed things up. It means wait for love and commitment to grow together.

That's so hard for us girls to do! We tend to scheme and plot and finagle to get a guy to like us, don't we? Just take a look at how many books, movies, and TV shows have plot lines that focus on "catching that man." Or the tremendous number of magazine headlines that promise to help us "win our guy." We devote a lot of time and energy to figuring out the best way to laugh, joke, charm, and flirt in order to hook a man and reel him in. All's fair in love and war, right? Actually, no.

See, that's not God's way. God wants you to let love "sleep" until he decides to awaken it—with the right guy, at the right time, in the right way. God wants you to concentrate on getting to know a guy, without expectations, and waiting on God to see what he brings about naturally. And if God does turn your friendship into something more, then he doesn't want you to rush things. Even then you need to let God dictate the pace.

God wants you to guard your heart, your mind, and your body—so that they belong to him first and eventually to your future husband. Chances are you're a long way from marriage at your age—so take it slow. Enjoy your relationships and don't be in such a hurry to get to the next stage in love and life. God's given you plenty to enjoy right now, right where you are.

 CHECK OUT SONG OF SONGS 2:3-13 FOR AN EXAMPLE OF HOW GREAT REAL LOVE IS WHEN YOU LET IT DEVELOP NATURALLY AND WAIT FOR IT TO UNFOLD IN GOD'S TIMING.

>> *God, you know that when I've got a crush, it's hard to sit back and focus on the friendship and let you do what you want with it. Help me to trust that you know what's best for me far more than I do...*

High Security

We all own things that we treat with special care—such as an expensive suede jacket, diamond necklace, or favorite photo album. Well, your heart is far more precious and valuable than your most treasured possession. (And by *heart* we don't mean that vital organ pumping blood in your chest. By *heart* we mean *you*—the real you, your person, the inner you.)

One day God may bring a special guy into your life who will treasure your heart for the rest of his life. Wouldn't it be nice to give him your whole heart rather than the "leftovers"—small pieces that you didn't give away to other guys (who battered and bruised most of your heart)?

You can do that by choosing now to guard your heart (even if you've been stung emotionally in the past—God can restore you). Here are practical ways to do just that:

1. *Be picky about the guys in your life.* Don't even think about getting involved with a guy who's anything less than great—according to God's criteria. A guy who puts God first in his

life will also want what's best for you rather than taking from you whatever satisfies him.

2. *Guard your thoughts.* Sometimes we girls fall into sappy-romantic "I want a boyfriend" thoughts, watching love-story movies that don't reflect God's standards (or even reality, for that matter). These types of media—love songs, cheap romance novels, even fashion magazines—can feed us unhealthy ideas of what true love is.

3. *When you do have a boyfriend, make sure you have a life apart from him.* Don't spend every waking minute together. Continue to invest in your friendships. Stay involved in whatever activities interest you—even if they don't interest him. Don't lose your personality to your relationship!

4. *Invest deeply in your relationship with God.* Make sure God has your heart. Share your thoughts and feelings, hopes and dreams, fears, and insecurities with the one who already knows them all. Make God your first, last, and truest love.

Use your head to guard your heart.

 FOR MORE PRACTICAL WISDOM THAT WILL HELP YOU GUARD YOUR HEART, READ PROVERBS 4:10-27.

 Father, I'm so glad you know my heart! Give me wisdom to know how to watch over it...

The Not-So-Perfect Guy

Do not be yoked together with unbelievers. For what
do righteousness and wickedness have in common?
Or what fellowship can light have with darkness?

2 Corinthians 6:14

Gorgeous. Smart. Popular. Athletic. Hilarious. And interested in you. Sounds like the perfect guy, doesn't it?

Not so fast, sister. You've left out the most important detail: *Is this guy a Christian?* Paul says believers weren't meant to blend with unbelievers—just like oil and water won't mix, no matter how hard you try. This doesn't mean you shouldn't have friendships with non-Christians. But it does mean you need to steer clear of closely uniting yourself with someone who doesn't follow Christ—especially when it comes to dating and marriage.

Here's what Paul means when he says not to be "yoked together with unbelievers": In Paul's day, two animals were commonly harnessed (or yoked) together to pull a plow. If you yoked two different kinds of animals together, they would pull unevenly or in different directions—often with disastrous results. In the same way, binding a nonbeliever and a believer can have devastating effects. If you follow Jesus and your guy doesn't, then your lives are heading in completely different directions. Either you'll wind up compromising your

Christian commitment or standards, or you'll end up with a broken heart. It's a lose-lose situation.

Many a girl has believed she could change a non-Christian guy; that by dating him she would be able to better witness to him. It's called "missionary dating." And it's often a recipe for disaster. If you're truly meant to be with this guy, then you can wait for him to become a Christian.

Many girls also believe that because a guy calls himself a Christian, goes to church, or is interested in God, then that must mean he's genuinely a believer. But many people call themselves Christians or go to church without truly following Jesus, and being interested in God doesn't necessarily mean you've given your life to him.

So before you get involved with a guy, you have to know whether or not he's really a Christian. If he is, great! Then you can evaluate other factors (similar interests, compatible personalities, etc.) before making a final decision. But if he's not, be a friend and pray that he becomes one—whether you end up dating or not!

 READ THE REST OF PAUL'S WARNINGS ABOUT HOOKING UP WITH UNBELIEVERS IN 2 CORINTHIANS 6:14-7:1.

 God, I know some great guys who don't know you. Help me hold out for a guy who will love both me and you...

The Best-Dressed-Girl Award

I also want women to dress modestly, with decency and propriety, not with braided hair or gold or pearls or expensive clothes, but with good deeds, appropriate for women who profess to worship God.

1 Timothy 2:9-10

Does this verse mean I should trash my hair clips, sell my jewelry, and start shopping at a thrift store? Well, that's not really the point here. So what is? Paul means that what gets you noticed shouldn't be your outward appearance; it should be your heart. It should be the love you show for others, which is a reflection of your love for God. If something about you really grabs people's attention, it should be your character—not how great you look in your pricey outfit.

Think about how much time you spend on your appearance when you want to get a guy's attention. You choose your clothes carefully and do your best to make sure your hair and makeup look perfect. You put some serious thought and effort into looking your best.

But how much thought and effort do you put into making your heart beautiful? How often do you think about developing godly character? A high-quality guy is looking for a girl with more to her than her appearance. He may appreciate your outer beauty, but it's going to be your heart that wins him over.

So focus on beautifying your heart. Carefully choose what's going to be most important to you. Do your best to make sure your love for God and for others is growing. And in the end, if you have a choice between being known as the best-dressed girl in school or being known as a girl who's tight with God, you'll know which you *should* choose—but will you?

GOD'S NOT IMPRESSED BY EXTERNALS; WE SHOULDN'T BE, EITHER. CHECK OUT 1 PETER 3:3-6 AND JAMES 2:1-9 FOR MORE ON VALUING INTERNAL BEAUTY OVER EXTERNAL APPEARANCES.

›› › *God, I'm so glad you care more about what's on the inside than what's on the outside. Help me to have your perspective on my appearance. Help me focus more of my energies on what's most important to you—my heart...*

True Love

> Love is patient, love is kind. It does not envy, it does not boast, it is not proud. It is not rude, it is not self-seeking, it is not easily angered, it keeps no record of wrongs. Love does not delight in evil but rejoices with the truth. It always protects, always trusts, always hopes, always perseveres.
>
> 1 Corinthians 13:4-7

When you think about being in love, what comes to mind? Moonlit nights, starry-eyed gazes? Love is far more than romantic feelings. And it's not something you "fall" in and out of. Genuine love is a *decision* to act a certain way, regardless of how you *feel*. Love is patient when you're frustrated, kind when others are unkind. Love always seeks the good in the other person. Love doesn't get mad easily or hold grudges. Love is trusting, protective, hopeful, and strong.

We throw around the word *love* to mean all kinds of things. *I love chocolate. I love your new jeans. I'd love to hang out.* In most situations, other words are actually more accurate—words such as *like, appreciate, enjoy, admire, find attractive.* Perhaps we need to reclaim the word *love* and save it for where it really applies. We need to resist the tendency to throw it around casually.

Let's face it—our words often reflect our hearts. And it's important that in our hearts we don't confuse true love with other things.

You may be attracted to a guy, like him a ton, have a great deal of affection for him, be completely and totally infatuated with him—but be careful not to confuse that with love.

True love will stand the test of time. It will always protect, always trust, always hope, always persevere. Would you say that you've been "in love" before? Would you say that you're "in love" right now? Make sure you think and pray hard about the way you think and talk about love.

 YOU WANT TO LEARN MORE ABOUT TRUE LOVE? THEN READ 1 CORINTHIANS 13:1-13.

>> *God, it seems like everybody's definition of* love *is different. Help me to view love from your perspective, to define it the way you do. Keep me from confusing love with other things...*

It's a Gift

> You are a garden locked up, my sister, my bride;
> you are a spring enclosed, a sealed fountain.
>
> Song of Songs 4:12

Wow! If you read these verses in Song of Songs, you'll see that this guy is head-over-heels in love—deep, passionate, lasting, till-death-do-us-part love. You'll see that he absolutely adores his bride. And isn't that what every girl dreams of? Now if you look closely at the things he praises her for, you'll see that her virginity is one of them. He calls her "a garden locked up," "a spring enclosed, a sealed fountain"—all beautiful things that are hidden away—and he loves that about her!

Unfortunately, many people don't value virginity the way God does. In fact, they view being a virgin as a negative thing, like it's some kind of failure or defect. Somehow they mistakenly equate "losing your virginity" with either winning a prize or conquering an obstacle. But sex outside of marriage is neither of those things. From God's perspective, it's a tragedy, not a victory. (And if you've experienced that tragedy, then you know just how painful and disappointing it can be.)

It's vitally important for you to recognize and remember that the world's view of virginity and God's view of virginity are diametrically opposed. God views virginity as a gift; the world views it as a liability. And if you've lost that gift, then remember that it's never too late to pledge yourself to stay pure from now on. God is a God of second chances! He can and will make you pure again.

While some people may put you down for wanting to stay a virgin until marriage, the right man—the one who really counts—will love that about you. Remember *that* when you're being made fun of for being a virgin or when you wonder if you're missing out on something. Remember *him*—the future love of your life—and the God who made you and loves you both.

CHECK OUT MORE OF THE INTIMATE DETAILS OF SOLOMON'S LOVE FOR HIS BRIDE IN SONG OF SONGS 4:1-15. (REMEMBER, WHILE SOME OF THE POETIC COMPLIMENTS MAY SOUND WEIRD TO YOU, THEY WOULD HAVE MADE A HEBREW GIRL BLUSH CLEAR DOWN TO HER TOES!)

God, it's easy to think the way the world thinks and be embarrassed about being a virgin. Help me hold on to your truth and protect this gift you've given me for my future husband...

Run, Girl, Run!

Flee from sexual immorality...Do you not know that your body is a temple of the Holy Spirit, who is in you, whom you have received from God? You are not your own; you were bought at a price. Therefore honor God with your body.

1 Corinthians 6:18-20

"It's *my* body. I can do what I want with it." You'll hear that message a lot from other girls, celebrities, in magazines, on TV. And even though you hear it from so many different places, you need to know this: *It's not true.*

When you belong to God, your body is not your own. God purchased you with Jesus' life, so he owns your body. Your body houses the Spirit of God. And it's important to God that you keep his temple pure. So contrary to popular opinion, you can't just do whatever you want with your body.

And that's especially true when it comes to sex. Did you notice what God says to do in relation to sexual immorality? He doesn't say you should avoid it if possible. He doesn't say you should just make sure you have good reasons for it. He doesn't say it's fine to flirt with it as long as you don't cross a certain line. He says to *flee* from it. Make tracks. Hightail it outta there. God wants you to do your best to run in the opposite direction of sexual immorality—by moving hard and fast toward sexual purity. *That* honors God and protects you. So wherever you've been, whatever you've done, whether sexual purity has been a breeze or a battle for you—start running now toward sexual purity.

It doesn't matter what anyone else says. It's not your body—it's God's. And he cares a great deal about what you do with it. Choose to honor him by keeping yourself sexually pure.

 SEE MORE OF HOW IMPORTANT SEXUAL PURITY IS TO GOD WHEN YOU READ 1 CORINTHIANS 6:9-20. (YOU CAN ALSO CHECK OUT 1 THESSALONIANS 4:3-8.)

>> *God, I thank you for the extraordinary price you paid for me when you sent your Son to die on the cross. Remind me that I belong to you and help me to honor you completely with my heart, soul, mind, and body...*

Day after Day

After a while his master's wife took notice of Joseph and said, "Come to bed with me!" But he refused..."How then could I do such a wicked thing and sin against God?" And though she spoke to Joseph day after day, he refused to go to bed with her or even to be with her.

Genesis 39:7-10

Day after day. Did you catch that? Potiphar's wife tried to seduce Joseph day after day. And *every* time Joseph chose to stay sexually pure. He believed that to do otherwise would be to sin against God. Joseph loved God enough to run from temptation day after day.

There are many good reasons for abstinence: wanting to be loved for more than just your body, avoiding sexually transmitted diseases and unwanted pregnancies, wanting to form deeper relationships that don't involve sex, wanting to enter marriage free from the pain and baggage of sexual memories. The list goes on and on.

Like Joseph, you will probably face ongoing pressure. It may come from your friends, your boyfriend, or your own desires or insecurities. Whatever form it takes, you have to be prepared to stand up to it—each and every time.

God doesn't require abstinence because he wants to see you suffer. Or because he wants to keep you from enjoying something good. Or because he doesn't understand the dynamics between guys and girls. God requires it because he wants what's best for you. When God says "no," what he means is "don't hurt yourself." He wants you to enjoy the very best that life offers.

Every day you face the same choice Joseph did. Will *you* honor God in your sexual choices? Joseph's choice brought him trouble (prison!) at first, and maybe he wondered if it was worth it. But God overwhelmingly blessed his right choice—and he'll do the same for you.

 THERE'S SO MUCH TO JOSEPH'S STORY! READ MORE ABOUT HIS TEMPTATION AND THE RESULTS OF HIS CHOICE IN GENESIS 39:1-23.

 God, I know you only want the best for me. Help me stand firm in obeying you each and every time I'm tempted to give in...

Complete Stain Removal

Have mercy on me, O God, according to your unfailing love. Wash away all my iniquity and cleanse me from my sin. Cleanse me with hyssop, and I will be clean; wash me, and I will be whiter than snow.

Psalm 51:1a, 2, 7

Ahhh, there's nothing like a long, hot shower to make you feel clean. But there are some things you can't clean, no matter how many showers you take. Maybe you've tried. You've stood in the shower, turned up the water as hot as you could possibly stand, and tried to scrub your guilt away. And yet you still feel dirty.

If you've blown it sexually, no matter what pleasure you gained in the moment, the Holy Spirit at work in your life will convict you of your sin. You'll feel that tremendous sense of guilt. You'll feel dirty and stained in a way that can't be scrubbed away by anyone but God.

Actually, that's step #1 of God's stain-removal process: He makes you aware of the problem. Then you have to make a crucial choice. You can try to ignore the guilt and hope it goes away—which might work for a while but not forever. You can wallow in the guilt—and then miss seeing God's way out of it. You can try to "be a better person"—though it's humanly impossible to be "good enough."

Or you can follow step #2 of God's stain-removal process: Ask God to cleanse you. Confess your sin to God, knowing that he forgives you the moment you ask. God is able to remove your sin completely, no matter how dark it is—leaving you white as snow.

You can never get back your virginity once you've given it away. But you can experience the joy of having your relationship with God restored after you confess your sin. You can experience the refreshment of being washed clean from the guilt and stain of your sin. God can make your soul pure again.

 FIND ENCOURAGEMENT IN DAVID'S CONFESSION OF SIN AND HIS EXPERIENCE WITH GOD'S CLEANSING WHEN YOU READ PSALM 51:1-17.

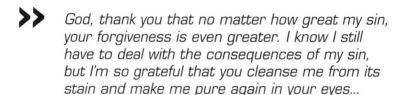 *God, thank you that no matter how great my sin, your forgiveness is even greater. I know I still have to deal with the consequences of my sin, but I'm so grateful that you cleanse me from its stain and make me pure again in your eyes...*

You Want Great Sex?

I belong to my lover, and his desire is for me.

Song of Songs 7:10

Our culture's obsessed with having the best sex possible. You can get all kinds of sex advice from television, magazines, books, and other people. But if you really want to know how to have extraordinary sex, then you'd better check with the inventor: God.

He designed sex. It's going to work best—and you'll get the most from it—when you follow his design. God designed sex to mysteriously unite a husband and wife. If you have sex outside of marriage, it "binds" you to that other person, and when your relationship ends, you lose a part of yourself that you can never get back. (But remember: if you've sinned or have been sinned against sexually, you can ask for God's 100 percent whole-body/soul/mind restoration and a fresh start sexually. From now on, you *can* save yourself for your husband.)

Our culture claims that hot sex happens outside of marriage, while sex between a husband and wife gets boring. FALSE! In order to give your whole heart and body to another person, you have to trust that person completely. The hottest sex happens within the security of a committed marriage.

Then you don't have to worry whether you'll be "good at it" your first time. You have years to practice together and perfect it. Then you don't have to worry whether your boyfriend is comparing you to another girl. Then you don't have to worry that all he wants is sex. He's made a commitment to stick around.

It's time for us to get rid of all the distorted ideas we have about sex and reclaim God's view of sex. Within marriage it's an amazing bond that God will bless.

 You want to see what you've got waiting for you if you wait? Read Song of Songs 7:1-8:6.

>> *God, help me see sex from your perspective—to know that it's a great thing, but only if I do it your way and in your time. Help me not to get caught up in the world's view of sex...*

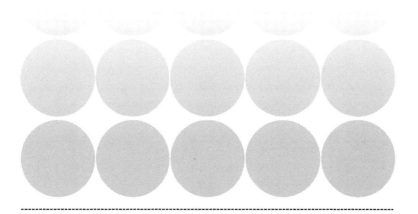

Section 10

R-E-S-P-E-C-T!

Gotta Live with 'Em

Children, obey your parents in the Lord, for this is right.
"Honor your father and mother"—which is the first
commandment with a promise—"that it may go well with
you and that you may enjoy long life on the earth."

Ephesians 6:1-3

Parents...you can't live with 'em; you can't live without 'em. Of course, at this point you have no choice—you have to live with them. More than that, you have to obey and honor them. And sometimes that's easier said than done, isn't it?

You're probably well aware that your parents aren't perfect. Even the best parents don't get it right all the time. God says that no matter what—even when they fail or make mistakes—you still need to honor your parents. Your respect for them doesn't depend on their actions; it depends on their God-given position as your parents. You need to respect their authority in your life no matter how good or bad a job you think they're doing.

If you want to be a girl who obeys God, then obey your parents. It's no mistake that you have the parents you do. God matched you up with them for a purpose, which you may or may not be able to see. God knew that you could bring him glory as the daughter of your particular mom and dad—with their particular strengths, weaknesses, personalities, rules, and convictions.

You may not agree with your parents on everything. And that's okay. But you must still respect and honor them, which means more than just going through the motions of doing what they tell you. It means having an attitude that respects their advice and that's grateful for the ways God uses them.

Notice this command comes with a promise: *That it may go well with you.* God put your parents in your life for a reason—with your good in mind. So apart from abusive behavior, don't struggle against your parents. Yield to their authority, trust God to work through them, and you'll enjoy the blessings of obedience in your life.

 READ ABOUT MORE OF THE WAYS GOD WANTS US TO HONOR OTHERS IN A VARIETY OF RELATIONSHIPS IN EPHESIANS 5:21-6:9.

 God, sometimes my parents drive me crazy! I know I need some help with my attitude. Help me to truly honor them in my heart and in my actions...

Like They Know Anything

But Rehoboam rejected the advice the elders gave him and consulted the young men who had grown up with him and were serving him.

1 Kings 12:8

Rehoboam became king when his father, Solomon, died. His royal subjects asked the new king to make some changes. Rehoboam asked his father's advisers what to do, and they wisely suggested that he grant the people's request. But he didn't like their advice, so he asked his buddies. His proud young friends encouraged him to show who was boss and deny the people's plea. Instead of listening to his elders, he listened to his friends. And the results were disastrous—the people rebelled, and his kingdom split.

When you need advice, where do you turn? Most girls naturally turn to their friends. They either whip out their cell phones or go on-line. And hours later, when they finally hang up the phones or log off the computers, and their moms stick their heads in their rooms and ask what's up, they shrug and say, "Nothing."

Nothing? Some girls might spill it all to Mom, and a few might unload on Dad, but many girls wouldn't think of sharing their "personal" issues with their parents. Parents, teachers, pastors—they may not be the people you'd ask for advice *dead last,* but they're probably not the *first.*

Why not? Granted the adults in your life may not have good fashion advice. But the life issues you struggle with now are the same issues they struggled with. They can remember what it feels like to be rejected by a crush, to do something stupid to fit in, and to be confused or insecure about what's important in life.

Instead of being your last resort, the trusted adults in your life should be your first resort for help. They *do* know what it feels like to go through what you're going through, and you can learn from both their mistakes and their successes. They can step back and see beyond the moment to the big picture—and that makes their advice invaluable.

 CHECK OUT AN EXAMPLE OF WHAT *NOT* TO DO WHEN YOU READ ABOUT REHOBOAM'S FOOLISHNESS IN 1 KINGS 12:1-15.

 God, sometimes I blow off the adults in my life. It just seems so natural to talk to my friends. But help me to value the wisdom and advice from people of all ages...

The Rebel Within

Submit yourselves for the Lord's sake to every authority
instituted among men. Show proper respect to everyone:
Love the brotherhood of believers, fear God, honor the king.

1 Peter 2:13a, 17

You may not enjoy submitting to the authorities in your life. When
your parents tell you to clean your room, maybe you roll your eyes
and complain. When your coach asks you to play a different position, maybe you make it very clear to her how you feel. When your
youth pastor wants you to work out your problems with another girl
at church, maybe you just avoid them both.

But the authorities in your life are not the enemy. The whole
rebel thing is overrated. God put people in authority over you for
your own good. He put them there to protect and provide for you.
When you fight against them, you're not doing yourself any favors.

God works through your parents, teachers, pastors, police, and
even politicians! When you disagree with them, you should do it re-
spectfully. You should submit to their authority whether you feel like
it or not. Just because you think your curfew's ridiculously early, or it
seems like everybody else ignores the legal drinking age, or you feel
like it's a stupid place for a stop sign—you need to submit to those

rules because it shows that you respect not only human authorities, but also God.

Respecting authorities will reflect in your actions—what you do. It will be seen in your attitudes—what comes through behind your deeds. And it will be heard in your words—the things you say and how you say them. Do you badmouth your parents or teachers or complain about their rules? Do you push the limits and see just how much you can get away with? Do you obey on the outside while you're rebelling on the inside? It's time to stop fighting against what God provided for your good.

 BELONGING TO GOD MEANS RESPECTING THE AUTHORITIES IN YOUR LIFE. READ MORE ABOUT WHAT IT MEANS TO BELONG TO GOD AND WHAT HE EXPECTS FROM HIS PEOPLE IN 1 PETER 2:9-3:7.

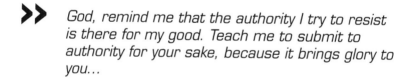

God, remind me that the authority I try to resist is there for my good. Teach me to submit to authority for your sake, because it brings glory to you...

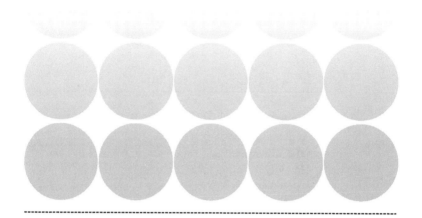

Section 11

Share the Love

Just a Touch

A man with leprosy came and knelt before [Jesus] and said, "Lord, if you are willing, you can make me clean." Jesus reached out his hand and touched the man. "I am willing," he said. "Be clean!" Immediately he was cured of his leprosy.

Matthew 8:2-3

In Jesus' day, no one touched lepers. Ever. No one hugged them, shook their hands, or even brushed against them in a crowd. Lepers had a contagious skin disease and lived separately from everyone else to prevent the disease from spreading. According to Jewish law they were "unclean," so they were completely excluded from all activities in the community. They lived in isolation and shame—complete outcasts in society.

This leper took a huge risk, braving the crowds to see Jesus. He knew everyone else would reject him, but he had enough faith to risk coming to Jesus. And Jesus healed him. But did you see what happened first, before the healing? Jesus *touched* him.

Jesus didn't have to do that, you know. Jesus healed many, many people with just a word. He didn't need to touch the leper to heal him. And he even touched the leper while he still had the disease—*wow*! Jesus showed incredible compassion, as he did what no one else would've dared do. Just think what it meant to the leper to have Jesus touch him! It may have been years—even decades—since any person had touched him. He must have been craving human touch, and Jesus more than met his need.

Can you think of someone who's treated like a leper—isolated, left out, excluded? Think how much it would mean to that person if you reached out in kindness. Others might think you're crazy and say, "Why would you ever eat lunch with her? She's so weird!" Reaching out might require some time and energy. It might feel awkward or uncomfortable. It might mean sacrificing some of your own status or popularity. But because Jesus went the extra mile, so should you. How will you show love and compassion to someone who especially needs it?

 CHECK OUT JESUS "THE HEALER" IN ACTION IN MATTHEW 8:1-17.

 God, I'd often prefer to stay in my comfort zone. It's hard to reach out. Remind me of your love and compassion and help me go the extra mile to show that to others who need it...

Look Out for the Underdog

Learn to do right! Seek justice, encourage the oppressed. Defend the cause of the fatherless, plead the case of the widow.

Isaiah 1:17

The people of Israel believed they were doing the "right" things. They fasted. They offered sacrifices. They knew the right religious lingo. They had religion down to a science, or so they thought. And they thought that as long as they went through the motions, God would be satisfied. Boy, were they wrong!

See, God doesn't care how religious we look. He's not impressed if we go to church three times a week and win the perfect attendance award at youth group. He cares about our motives and our genuine love for him. And that love should result in our showing justice, compassion, kindness, and real help to those who need it desperately. The Bible reveals that God has a special concern for the oppressed and needy. You could say that he's actually *obsessed* with caring for the poor and needy, for those without parents, for wives without husbands. These are the vulnerable ones in our society, the ones who often struggle just to make it through the day. And because God cares so deeply for them, we should, too.

Look around you. Who do you know who's hurting? A friend whose parents are getting divorced. An acquaintance who just lost a loved one. The new girl in class everyone makes fun of. The single mom from church who has no one to help her babysit or run errands. God tells us to help these people. Their wounds are raw, so we're to show them extra love.

What can you do to reach out? Write a card to tell them you care. Invite them to lunch, a movie, or just for a walk. Send flowers. Stand up for them when others put them down. Listen. Share. Offer practical help for their practical needs (like babysitting or doing yard work for free). Look for ways to give without expecting anything in return. God always looks out for the underdog. Do you?

 DON'T MISS THE POINT, AS ISRAEL DID. SEE WHAT'S REALLY IMPORTANT TO GOD IN ISAIAH 58:1-12.

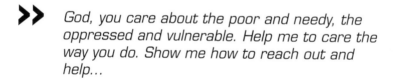 *God, you care about the poor and needy, the oppressed and vulnerable. Help me to care the way you do. Show me how to reach out and help...*

Meet My Friend

Andrew, Simon Peter's brother, was one of the two who heard what John had said and who had followed Jesus. The first thing Andrew did was to find his brother Simon and tell him, "We have found the Messiah" (that is, the Christ). And he brought him to Jesus.

John 1:40-42a

Did you notice the *first thing* Andrew did after following Jesus? He found his brother, told him about Jesus, and brought him to meet Jesus. If he'd had a cell phone, he would have called Simon right away. If he'd had a computer, he'd have instant messaged him. This news was so incredible that it just couldn't wait. And because he loved his brother, Andrew wanted to share the Good News with him ASAP.

Sometimes we make sharing the gospel far more complicated than it needs to be. We're worried we won't phrase it just right. We're afraid other people will have questions we can't answer. We think we need to be saved for a certain length of time before we'll be "ready" or "qualified" to talk to others about our faith.

Apparently Andrew didn't get that memo. He met Jesus and turned right around and told his brother about it. He didn't use a long list of theological arguments. He just said, "He's what we've been looking for." He did the best thing he could do—he brought his brother straight to Jesus.

If you have friends who need to meet Jesus, don't overcomplicate things. Just introduce your friends to your Savior. Talk openly and simply about who Jesus is and what he's done in your life. Invite them to church to hear the teachings of Jesus. And trust God to work through your efforts.

Have you chosen to follow Jesus? Have you shared that decision with the people you care about? Don't wait—get on it!

 READ ABOUT ANDREW'S "WITNESSING STRATEGY" IN JOHN 1:35-42. (YOU CAN SEE MORE PLACES WHERE ANDREW BROUGHT OTHER PEOPLE TO JESUS IN JOHN 6:5-9 AND 12:20-22.)

 God, I haven't wanted to talk to my friends about being a Christian because I don't know what to say. I still don't know for sure, but I want to do it anyway. Show me what I can do to introduce my friends to you...

No Hiding

> The word of the LORD came to Jonah son of Amittai:
> "Go to the great city of Nineveh and preach against it,
> because its wickedness has come up before me." But
> Jonah ran away from the LORD and headed for Tarshish.
>
> Jonah 1:1-3a

If you looked it up on a map, you'd find that Tarshish wasn't exactly on the way to Nineveh. Actually it was more like in the complete *opposite* direction! What was Jonah's deal?

The Ninevites were _____ (fill in the blank: harsh, cruel, evil, mean, etc.). So you'd expect that Jonah didn't want to go there because he was scared of what they might do to him, or scared they wouldn't listen. Actually, Jonah was more afraid that they *would* listen.

See, like most Israelites, Jonah hated the Ninevites. He wanted to see them punished for what they'd done. He wanted them to experience a portion of the pain they'd inflicted on others. He didn't mind preaching judgment against them. He just didn't want them to turn from their sin, because he knew that God is merciful and compassionate and would forgive them if they repented. And Jonah didn't want that to happen.

It's hard to see your enemies the way God does. It's hard to think of showing compassion to someone who's hurt you. But don't forget that you didn't deserve the mercy that God has shown you. No one deserves God's forgiveness and grace, but he gives it anyway. And he often wants us to be part of that process. We might try to run from our responsibility, but we can never run far enough to escape it.

Who's the "Ninevite" in your life? Is there someone who torments you, makes your skin crawl, drives you crazy? Give that person a shock and reach out to her. She might be so surprised that she'll actually consider what you have to say.

 READ ABOUT HOW JONAH TRIED TO RUN FROM SHARING GOD'S MESSAGE IN JONAH 1:1-17. (YOU CAN ALSO READ ABOUT JONAH'S MISGUIDED ANGER AT GOD'S COMPASSION IN JONAH 4:1-11!)

>> *God, I can't believe that you want me to share the gospel with _____ (go on, fill in a name!). Change my heart and remind me that I didn't deserve salvation, either. Give me the grace to do what you want me to do...*

Common Ground

Let's say you discovered a miraculous drink that completely satisfied your thirst and caused you to live forever. If you offered it to some friends but served it in a rusted-out old hubcap, they'd probably refuse. No matter how great you claimed it was, they'd be hesitant to drink it from the disgusting cup you offered it in. If you really wanted people to try this drink and discover for themselves that it's everything you said it is, then you'd need to put it into something that appeals to them.

If you were really savvy, you'd even choose the cup to fit the person. For your tea-loving grandmother, you'd offer it to her in a delicate china teacup. For your artsy mom, you'd put it in a funky pottery mug. For your athletic brother, you'd offer it in a sports bottle. For your baby sister, you'd put it in a sippy cup. You wouldn't change the drink at all, but you'd change the cup you served it in.

That's what Paul's talking about in this passage. His single most important goal in life was to share the gospel. So he took the message to others wherever they happened to be. That doesn't mean he compromised his identity or his message to please his listeners. It means he appealed to their common ground. He varied the style of his message and the way he presented it in order to better relate to those he shared it with.

Do you have a friend who loves sports like you do? Then start there. Have a friend who has a broken family like yours? You can relate. Know a girl who enjoys the same hobbies? Ha! You just found more common ground! Take the message to others—wherever they may be.

 CHECK OUT PAUL'S PERSPECTIVE ON DOING HIS BEST TO PREACH THE GOSPEL TO EVERYONE IN 1 CORINTHIANS 9:19-27.

 God, I want to share the gospel with others, but I don't always know where to start. Show me the common ground you've already given us. Help me to use that as a platform to share in a way that others will relate to...

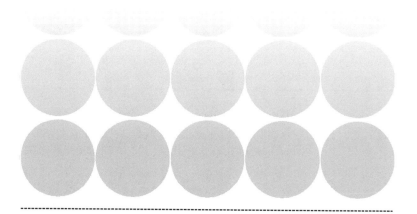

Section 12

Your New Identity

Me, a Princess?

Most little girls dream about being princesses. There's something about a princess that captures our imaginations. We dream about the royal castle, the extravagant clothes, and, of course, the handsome prince. We're drawn to the importance of the position, the distinctive place a princess holds in the kingdom. Maybe we wish we could be daughters of a king, too.

If you're a Christian, then your wish has come true! You were born as a slave to sin in Satan's dark kingdom, but God paid a high price—Jesus' life—to rescue you and bring you into his kingdom. You went from nobody to somebody special! You went from obscurity to the apple of the King's eye (Psalm 17:8). You became his adopted daughter, and that makes you a princess—with all the privileges and responsibilities that come along with that coveted title.

Every girl has to think through questions about her identity. The most important question you have to answer in life is *Who is God?* The next most important question is *Who am I?* You have to correctly answer #1 before you can even get close on #2. Only when you have a right view of God can you understand yourself and your identity clearly. Once you understand that he's the King of the universe, you'll see how lucky you are to be his daughter—which is what makes you significant.

Don't let anyone make you believe you aren't valuable. Because you belong to the King, you have great worth. God chose you to belong to him. You hold a distinctive place in his kingdom. You have a royal inheritance waiting for you in heaven. Find your identity in being a beloved daughter of the King of the universe.

 LEARN MORE ABOUT THE KING, HIS KINGDOM, AND YOUR PLACE IN IT IN COLOSSIANS 1:9-23.

 God, thank you that when you rescued me from sin, you made me your daughter. Help me to be aware of the privileges and responsibilities that come with being a princess in your kingdom...

Be the Moon

Bring my sons from afar and my daughters from the ends
of the earth—everyone who is called by my name, whom
I created for my glory, whom I formed and made.

Isaiah 43:6b-7

When you think about your future—choosing a college, pursuing a career, possibly getting married and starting a family—do you ever wonder what life is all about? What's the purpose of your time on earth? It seems like such a big, complicated question. But the answer is actually very simple: God created you for his glory. That's it. That's all there is to it. And you will find the truest satisfaction in life when you focus on that purpose.

You may unconsciously make the mistake of thinking that life is all about *you,* and maybe you pursue things that you think will fulfill you—then wonder why you feel so dissatisfied in life. Do you ever forget that life is about so much more than you?

It's easy to think and act as if the world revolves around you—as if you're the sun, this shining light beaming down on everyone else, as if you have something of your own to give. But the reality is that God is the sun, and you are the moon. On your own you have nothing to give. You simply reflect God's light. No matter how hard the moon tries, it can never be the sun.

So as you think about your life, remember that you're not here for yourself. The more you try to do your own thing and be the sun in your life and others' lives, the more dim and burned out you'll feel. But the more you make your life about God and live to reflect his light, his goodness, and his love to others, then the brighter your life will shine. Though the moon is always dim compared to the sun, it is beautiful *because of* the sun. So be the best moon you can be today.

 Learn more of God's purposes and plans for his people in Isaiah 43:1-13.

 God, it's so natural to want the world to revolve around me. Remind me that my life is supposed to be about bringing glory to you instead of to myself. Let my life reflect your light to the world around me...

Plain Old You

He grew up before him like a tender shoot, and like a root out of dry ground. He had no beauty or majesty to attract us to him, nothing in his appearance that we should desire him.

Isaiah 53:2

In our world there are "pretty people" and "not-so-pretty people." Everyone seems to get labeled as one or the other. If you're a pretty person, then it's easy to pin your worth on your good looks. People buzz around you like bees drawn to honey. And if you're not in that category, then it's easy to be jealous of the pretty people and wish you were one of them so that you'd feel more important.

But true beauty, value, and worth have *nothing* to do with your looks. (Read that sentence again 'til it soaks in.) Consider Jesus. You'd never find a more valuable man. In just a few years he changed the world, history, and eternity. He was the most influential person who ever lived—so you'd kind of expect that he was attractive, right? Actually, he wasn't. Isaiah says that Jesus had no beauty to attract other people to him. His appeal had nothing to do with his looks or his designer Jewish tunics. If you want a mental picture of him, imagine an average to homely-looking guy. But that didn't stop crowds of thousands of people from following him around and hanging on his every word. This guy was the real deal.

Isn't it nice to know that Jesus' strong appeal wasn't because of his good looks? Isn't it reassuring to know that it was his love, his message, and his miracles that drew people to him? This is comforting news because your value as a person has nothing to do with your looks, either. You're valuable because God created you, and you belong to him. Outside packaging is irrelevant. What makes you extraordinary is who you are on the inside.

 SEE THE INCREDIBLE THINGS THIS "UNATTRACTIVE" MAN—JESUS OUR SAVIOR—ACCOMPLISHED ON OUR BEHALF IN ISAIAH 53:1-12.

 Jesus, I'm glad you weren't a physically attractive guy. I'm even more glad that what makes you attractive is your heart. Help me to accept the way I look and focus instead on having an extraordinary heart, just like yours...

A World of Designer Dresses

I praise you because I am fearfully and wonderfully made;
your works are wonderful, I know that full well.

Psalm 139:14

Do you ever watch those Hollywood awards shows—you know, the Oscars, the Emmys, the Grammys? If so, then you know that half the appeal of the show has nothing to do with the awards or the celebrities themselves. Everyone's watching to see what the stars are *wearing*. Rarely do the stars show up wearing an off-the-rack dress that looks just like thousands of others in stores across the country. Oh no. This is a night of one-of-a-kind designer dresses—every one is unique and spectacular in its own way.

Did you know that every single person—including you!—is also a one-of-a-kind creation? You have been wonderfully created and formed by the Master Designer. You're no off-the-rack dress. You'll never run into another just like you. Uh-uh. You, my dear, are a Christian Dior, a Versace, an Oscar de la Renta. You reflect the handiwork of a highly talented, premier Designer.

So why compare yourself to other girls? You might think some girls are prettier, have cooler clothes, are more athletic, get better grades, get all the guys. (Of course, those girls are also looking around and seeing other girls who are prettier, more athletic, smarter, more popular...) The truth is that there's always someone better than you at something. Meanwhile, you're better at certain things than other girls. See how this comparison trap never ends? But it doesn't matter—because each of us is unique and special. You are a Versace while another girl is a Dior. No two alike, but both spectacular!

Yes, even the things you don't like about yourself, the things you wish you could change, are part of God's perfect plan. He doesn't make mistakes. So don't even go down that line of thinking. Remember that a perfect God made you perfectly—just the way you are.

 READ MORE OF HOW PRECIOUS YOU ARE TO THE GOD WHO CREATED THE MASTERPIECE CALLED "YOU" IN PSALM 139:13-18.

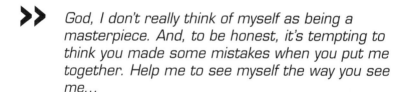 *God, I don't really think of myself as being a masterpiece. And, to be honest, it's tempting to think you made some mistakes when you put me together. Help me to see myself the way you see me...*

Let It Flow

For the grace of God that brings salvation has appeared to all men. It teaches us to say 'No' to ungodliness and worldly passions, and to live self-controlled, upright and godly lives in this present age.

Titus 2:11-12

Do you ever look around and feel like everyone else is just way more spiritual than you are? Maybe it feels as if they know something you don't or have some secret "in" with God that just naturally makes them "better" Christians. Like a senior girl who leads a Bible study on campus. Like your small group leader. Like your pastor. Maybe even your best friend. It's easy to start comparing yourself to them and wind up discouraged. It's easy to think, *I could never be a Christian like* that*!*

Pause. Time out. Let's think through this.

The grace of God that appeared to *all* people—including you—is the same grace that will help you grow in godliness. The same grace of God that saved superstar Christians also saved you. You have the same full-measure of grace at work in your life as they do in theirs. In time that grace will also teach you how to live a life of godliness—if you let it.

The only way to stunt your spiritual growth is to limit the flow of God's grace in your life. If God's working on you, you have to be ready and willing to cooperate! When he gives you the opportunity to say "no" to ungodliness, you have a choice: Do it God's way (through his grace) or do it your own way (rejecting his grace). If you say "yes" to sinful choices, then you block the flow of God's grace in your life. If you say "no" to sinful choices, then God's grace keeps flowing through your life.

So you see, your pastor has nothin' that you don't have! You've just got to keep growing and allowing God's grace to flow freely through your life.

 READ MORE ABOUT THE GRACE OF GOD THAT BELONGS TO YOU—JUST AS MUCH AS TO THE NEXT GIRL—IN TITUS 2:11-15.

 God, I want to let you work in my life. I want to keep growing in godliness and have a relationship with you that is solid and growing. Help me to allow your grace to flow in my life...

No Comparison

Let's face it: We constantly measure ourselves against others. We think, *I'm not so bad. At least I don't swear like Haley.* Or, *I'm better than Ashley because I actually read my Bible.* Or, *I might not be able to lead worship like Allie, but at least I'm nicer than she is.* But Jesus says not to get caught up in "comparative righteousness." Your standing before God isn't based on how good you are compared to someone else—it's based on whether or not you've placed your faith in Christ's perfect righteousness and his forgiveness.

You know, we generally compare ourselves to other people to boost our own egos. We want to find a way to feel better about ourselves by thinking that we're better than others. But that's a lame motive. That's pride and arrogance at work, and the comparison game just leads to even more pride and arrogance. If you want to compare yourself to someone else, then compare yourself to God. When you see how great God is and how small you are, it will boost your humility instead of your ego.

Jesus said that for every speck you see in someone else's eye, there's a two-by-four in your own eye (Matthew 7:3-5). We've all got our own issues—our own personal sets of sins, failures, and weaknesses. You have no right to look down on someone else and view yourself as any better. So quit pointing the finger; deal with your own issues instead. If you want to do some "constructive comparisons," take a good look at God and try to see yourself the way *he* sees you. Then try to see other people the way God sees them, too.

 FOR MORE WAYS TO FOCUS ON GOD, READ WHAT JESUS SAYS IN MATTHEW 7:1-27.

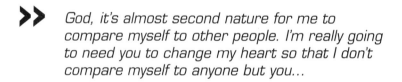 *God, it's almost second nature for me to compare myself to other people. I'm really going to need you to change my heart so that I don't compare myself to anyone but you...*

Creative Multiplication

When Jesus looked up and saw a great crowd coming toward him, he said to Philip, "Where shall we buy bread for these people to eat?" Another of his disciples, Andrew, Simon Peter's brother, spoke up, "Here is a boy with five small barley loaves and two small fish, but how far will they go among so many?"

John 6:5, 8-9

Ever feel like you don't have much to offer God? Maybe you don't see yourself as especially smart, athletic, outgoing, or talented—certainly not the kind of person who does memorable things for God. But you'd be surprised. Just look at what God did with one boy's sack lunch. He multiplied those loaves and fish until they fed thousands—with leftovers! That's God's way. He loves to take the little we bring and multiply it miraculously.

Just think what would have happened if the boy hadn't offered his lunch. What if he'd decided to hold it back because he didn't think it would make much of a difference, given the size of this problem? Or what if Andrew hadn't brought the boy to Jesus? What if he'd brushed the boy off? Well, God still would have found a way to take care of the people, but the boy and Andrew would have missed out on being part of the miracle.

You also have opportunities to be part of miracles. Maybe all you have to offer to a hurting friend is a hug or a note telling her that you're there for her—but God can take that small gesture and multiply it into a tidal wave of encouragement in her life. Maybe you feel strongly about the right to life for the unborn but think your lone voice won't make a difference—but every time you speak up lovingly, God may use what you say to change the life of someone who's listening.

God doesn't need you in order to do the miracle. But he'll let you in on what he's doing if you give him what little you have. Then you get the rush of being part of something amazing. So don't hold back—offer what you have, and watch how God multiplies it.

 READ THE WHOLE "MULTIPLICATION" STORY IN JOHN 6:1-14.

 God, sometimes I feel like I have so little to give. Remind me that you can multiply whatever I bring...

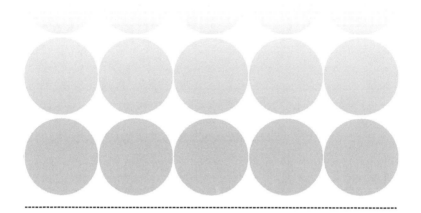

Section 13

Girl in Process

The Best-Dressed Award

Therefore, as God's chosen people, holy and dearly loved, clothe yourselves with compassion, kindness, humility, gentleness and patience...Forgive as the Lord forgave you. And over all these virtues put on love, which binds them all together in perfect unity.

Colossians 3:12-14

If you've put your faith in Jesus, then you have been chosen by God to belong to him. Remember, he's made you his daughter. And since he's the King, you're a princess. Don't you think it's important to dress the part?

If you're going to dress like a princess, the first thing you've got to do is get rid of what you wore before God adopted you. God says to take off the rags of sexual immorality, impurity, lust, evil desires, greed, anger, rage, malice, slander, filthy language, and lies (Colossians 3:5-9). That old wardrobe fit in fine in the kingdom of darkness where you used to live, but it's totally out of place in God's kingdom.

Instead, God wants your actions and attitudes to show that you are his daughter. He wants you to clothe yourself with a royal gown of compassion, kindness, humility, gentleness, patience, and forgiveness. And he wants you to tie it all together with love. When people look at your life, they should be able to tell that you belong to God. The character you "wear" should announce who you are.

This major wardrobe change doesn't just happen. We're so used to wearing those filthy old rags that we tend to put them on out of habit. So every day you have to choose to put on your new wardrobe. How? Try by starting your day off in prayer, asking God to help you develop those qualities. Read God's Word. Write out Colossians 3:12-14 and post those verses on your mirror to remind you to put on your "spiritual clothes" as you put on your physical ones. Aim for that best-dressed award!

 You can get more "spiritual wardrobe tips" when you read Colossians 3:5-17.

 God, thanks for making me your daughter. Help me to clothe myself every day in the new wardrobe you've given me—so I can be the girl you want me to be...

Fruit Salad, Please

But the fruit of the Spirit is love, joy, peace, patience, kindness, goodness, faithfulness, gentleness and self-control. Against such things there is no law.

Galatians 5:22-23

These verses aren't a to-do list. "I was kind today. I'll check that off. Tomorrow I'll work on self-control. Then I'll move on to patience." It's not like you work on one until you "get it right," then you move on to the next one. You know from experience that tomorrow you might not be very kind at all. The Holy Spirit is the one who produces fruit in your life, like grapes on a grapevine. The branch doesn't *decide* to grow grapes; it just does because it's connected to the vine.

Can you imagine a branch that wasn't connected to the vine, lying on the ground and still trying to bear fruit? It couldn't happen. In fact, before long that branch would wither and die. The only way to bear fruit is to stay connected to the vine.

So how do you stay connected to the vine? You stay tight with Jesus. You try to make decisions that will please him. You fill your mind with good things. You listen carefully to your conscience so you can hear the Spirit correcting and guiding you. These aren't one-time tasks. They're ongoing parts of a never-ending process. You learn to rely less and less on yourself and more and more on God.

As you do that, the Spirit of God grows fruit in your life. You'll see love, joy, peace, patience, kindness, goodness, faithfulness, gentleness, and self-control multiply in you. If you've always been an impatient person, you'll get to see God growing patience in you—something you know you never could have done on your own. And while you won't always have all of these qualities down perfectly, you'll have them more and more—a major fruit salad in the making!

 FOR MORE WAYS TO STAY CONNECTED TO THE VINE, CHECK OUT GALATIANS 5:13-26.

>> *God, thank you for your Spirit that's at work in me. Show me how to stay connected to you, the vine. Help me to depend on you so others will see the fruit of your Spirit at work in my life...*

Nothin' but the Best

Finally, brothers, whatever is true, whatever is noble, whatever is right, whatever is pure, whatever is lovely, whatever is admirable—if anything is excellent or praiseworthy—think about such things.

Philippians 4:8

When you shop for a big-ticket item, such as a digital camera or a computer, you probably don't buy the first one you stumble across. You want the very best, if you can get it. Most likely you shop around, ask some friends, and check out reviews and consumer reports so you can get an idea of the best buy. Maybe your motto is "nothin' but the best!" and it's worth a little extra time and effort to make sure you get it.

What about the books you read? The movies you watch? TV shows or music? Do you consider what is *the best*? What do you base that on? What kind of criteria do you use to decide what's best for your brain? Have you checked out God's "consumer report"—the Bible?

The Bible tells us that God's standard for what we put in our minds is nothing short of excellence. Whatever is *true*—accurate and faithful to God's perspective on life and the world. Whatever is *noble*—dignified and honest. Whatever is *right*—fair and trustworthy. Whatever is *pure*—clean and healthy. Whatever is *lovely*—charming and attractive. Whatever is *admirable*—highly regarded. Those words describe what God views as excellent and praiseworthy—that is, the very best.

In what areas have you been settling for less than the best for your mind? Let the motto for your brain also be "nothin' but the best!" Be picky about movies, TV shows, music, and magazines. Change your perspective from "Can I get away with watching this?" to "What will I gain from watching this?" It doesn't matter what everyone else around you is doing or not doing. It's up to you to monitor what fills your gray matter.

 READ PAUL'S ENCOURAGEMENT TO STAND FIRM IN PURSUING THE BEST IN PHILIPPIANS 4:1-9.

 God, I know there are some things in my life that don't fit the standards you gave me. I know they pull me down rather than build up my relationship with you. Help me to care enough about you to allow in only what you think is best...

So Many Choices

At Gibeon the LORD appeared to Solomon during the night in a dream, and God said, "Ask for whatever you want me to give you." [Solomon answered,] "So give your servant a discerning heart to govern your people and to distinguish between right and wrong. For who is able to govern this great people of yours?"

1 Kings 3:5,9

If you could have one wish granted, what would you ask for? Given just one wish, Solomon asked God for wisdom. Solomon knew he would have many difficult decisions and choices ahead of him, so he asked for the one thing that would help him most—God's wisdom.

You also have a ton of decisions and choices ahead of you. Choices about your time—like whether to play soccer or softball. Choices about your relationships—like who your friends will be and whether or not to date a certain guy. Choices about your image— like what kind of clothes you'll wear and how you'll style your hair. Choices about your future—like whether or not go to college, and if so, where.

You probably face decisions on whether or not to do drugs, drink, or smoke. You have choices to make about your sexuality—like whether to abstain from sex until marriage or how far to go with a guy sexually. And if you haven't already made the most important choice of all, you have to decide how to respond to Jesus—whether you'll give your life to him or try to muddle through life on your own.

While some choices are scarier than others, all of the choices you make are important in one way or another. The decisions you make today affect your future. If you want to be able to look back on your life without regrets, then don't underestimate the value of wise decisions. Go straight to the source—God—for the wisdom you need to make good choices today, tomorrow, and every day after that. You won't regret it.

 READ THE STORY OF SOLOMON'S "ONE WISH GRANTED" AND HOW HE IMMEDIATELY PUT HIS WISDOM INTO PRACTICE IN 1 KINGS 3:5-28.

 God, sometimes I love having choices to make, and sometimes it feels overwhelming. I want to turn to you for the wisdom I need to make good choices—in both the big and the small things of life...

Fruit-Check, Root-Check

The good man brings good things out of the good stored up in his heart, and the evil man brings evil things out of the evil stored up in his heart. For out of the overflow of his heart his mouth speaks.

Luke 6:45

When you see oranges on a tree, you can tell it's an orange tree. When you pick a peach, you know you found a peach tree. And if the fruit's diseased, blighted, small, or shriveled, then you can tell something's wrong with the tree. Yep, you can find out a lot about a tree by its fruit.

You know, you can also tell a lot about a girl's heart by what she says. That's because your words are the "fruit," or evidence, of what's in your heart. Petty, gossipy, snide comments reveal a jealous heart. Generous, encouraging words reveal a kind heart. What do your words reveal about you? Do you gush foolish words, say hurtful things, and spread gossip? Or do you speak the truth, say helpful things, and spread encouragement?

If you find that your words reveal some sin in your heart, then know that only part of the solution is watching what you say. No matter how hard you try to bite your tongue, if you have bitterness in your heart toward someone, that will eventually overflow from your heart through your mouth. You'll only be able to hold those bitter words back for so long. What you really have to do is deal with your heart.

After you say something you shouldn't have, dig down to find the roots. Was the comment rooted in jealousy of another person, your own pride or insecurity, bitterness, or hurt? Once you get to the root of the problem, then you can start dealing with it. You can confess your sin to God, ask him to change you, and turn from that attitude. You can fill your heart with good things so that they will overflow in your words. And every time you get ready to open that mouth of yours, think about what you're going to say...and what that says about you.

 READ MORE ABOUT THE KIND OF HEART THAT RESULTS IN SPEECH THAT PLEASES GOD IN LUKE 6:20-49.

 God, I know my words reveal some problems in my heart. Show me the root of the problem, and change me...

The Girl Who Makes God Smile

To some who were confident of their own righteousness and looked down on everybody else, Jesus told this parable: "Two men went up to the temple to pray, one a Pharisee and the other a tax collector."

Luke 18:9-10

Picture this: A "good" Christian girl stands in church and prays, "God, thank you that I'm not like other girls who sleep around, party, smoke, drink, and swear—like that tattoo-covered girl over there who'd probably hook up with anyone. What's *she* doing here?!" Meanwhile, the other girl, who was indeed guilty of all those things, prays tearfully, "God, have mercy on me, a sinner."

That's basically the same story as the one Jesus told in Luke 18. While Jesus' original version involved a Pharisee and a tax collector at the temple, the message of the story is the same. And it's a message you can't afford to miss.

See, Jesus told this story to people who thought they were better than everybody else. And sometimes we can have that same attitude. But in this story we get a close look at what matters to God. Even though the Pharisee had never done the same awful things as the tax collector, the Pharisee's prayer did not make him right with God. But the tax collector made God smile that day. That's because the tax collector recognized his sin, confessed it, and surrendered himself openly to the mercy of God.

The most important difference between the two men wasn't their actions; it was their hearts. One man exalted himself while the other humbled himself—and that made all the difference. Be honest; which do you do? If you were a girl in the first story, would you be patting yourself on the back for how good you are, or would you be surrendering yourself to the mercy of God? If you don't care for the answer, just remember that it's never too late to change roles. You, too, can be the girl who makes God smile.

JESUS TOLD MANY STORIES THAT HIGHLIGHT THE VALUE OF HUMILITY IN THE KINGDOM OF GOD. CHECK OUT SOME OF THEM IN LUKE 18:9-30.

God, once again I'm reminded that you care more about my heart than anything else. Give me humility to recognize my sin and trust in your mercy...

Hot

I know your deeds, that you are neither cold nor hot. I wish you were either one or the other! So, because you are lukewarm—neither hot nor cold—I am about to spit you out of my mouth.

Revelation 3:15-16

Let's say you go to the coffee shop and order a latté. Anticipating the piping hot warmth of your favorite drink, you take a sip and discover that it's not hot. It's lukewarm. Yuck! You're sending that one right back! Or say you order a frozen coffee, looking forward to the icy smoothness of the frosty drink, but your first taste reveals that it's also lukewarm. Gross! Totally unappealing, right?

Well, it's also totally unappealing to be lukewarm in your walk with God—to be without convictions, indifferent, not really caring about much of anything spiritually. That's the kind of thing that makes God sick. God doesn't do things halfway. He loved you full-on and full-out when he gave his Son for you. He wants that same kind of love and passion in return.

For many girls, being a Christian isn't a big deal. It's something they do on Sundays, it changes a few of the words they use, and it keeps them from getting into "hardcore" sins—that's about it. But God wants way more. He wants your Christianity to be a big deal—a huge deal, in fact. He wants your relationship with him to shape every area of your life. He wants fire, passion, and heat in your relationship with him. And if you're only willing to go as far as "lukewarm," it's really not worth it.

Jesus wants you to be completely sold-out for him. If you've been living in the middle, not willing to reject Jesus but not ready to fully embrace him either, then you're in a dangerous spot.

With God, it's all or nothing. It's time to turn up the heat, girl!

 CHECK OUT THE REST OF JESUS' WARNINGS TO THE LUKEWARM CHURCH IN LAODICEA WHEN YOU READ REVELATION 3:14-22.

 God, thank you for loving me so extravagantly. If I'm lukewarm in any way, Father, please ignite a fiery passion in me to love and serve you...

INTRODUCING THE ONLY NIV BIBLE SPECIFICALLY FOR TEEN GIRLS AGES 13-16. TRUE IMAGES COMBATS THE WORLD'S FALSE IMAGES BY POINTING GIRLS TO GOD'S MESSAGES ABOUT WHO THEY ARE, WHERE THEY ARE GOING, AND WHAT THEY ARE WORTH IN HIS EYES. THESE TRUE MESSAGES BRING LIFE, HOPE AND HAPPINESS BY HELPING THEM STRENGTHEN THEIR RELATIONSHIPS WITH GOD, FAMILY, FRIENDS, AND GUYS.

TRUE IMAGES HAS LOADS OF SPECIAL FEATURES AND AN INFORMATIVE WEB SITE WITH ADDITIONAL RESOURCES ON MANY OF THE FEATURE TOPICS, BIBLE READING PLANS, LINKS TO OTHER SITES AND MORE!

True Images SC
The NIV Bible for Teen Girls
Livingstone Corporation, General Editor

RETAIL $22.99
ISBN 0-310-92816-8

Visit www.invertbooks.com or your local bookstore.

SECRET POWER TO JOY IS ABOUT FINDING THE JOY ONLY GOD CAN GIVE. YOU'LL STUDY THE BOOK OF PHILIPPIANS AND LEARN GREAT STUFF ABOUT HOW THE HOLY SPIRIT HELPS BELIEVERS FIND REAL HAPPINESS DESPITE WHAT'S GOING ON IN THEIR LIVES OR ON THEIR HEADS.

Secret Power to Joy, Becoming a Star, and Great Hair Days
A Personal Bible Study on the Book of Philippians
Susie Shellenberger

RETAIL $9.99
ISBN 0-310-25678-X

THIS BOOK WILL HELP YOU FIGURE OUT WHAT DOES AND DOESN'T FIT WITH BEING A CHRISTIAN. YOU CAN DO THIS STUDY AT YOUR OWN PACE BY YOURSELF, WITH A FRIEND, OR WITH A BUNCH OF FRIENDS.

Secret Power to Treasures, Purity and a Good Complexion
A Personal Bible Study on the Book of Colossians
Susie Shellenberger

RETAIL $9.99
ISBN 0-310-25679-8

AUTHOR SUSIE SHELLENBERGER LEADS GIRL READERS, AGES 13 TO 17, ON AN ENGAGING EXPLORATION OF 1 PETER. THROUGH HER TRUE-TO-LIFE ANECDOTES AND FUN ASSIGNMENTS, STUDENTS WILL COME TO REALIZE THAT HAPPINESS AND SUCCESS COME BY DRESSING THEMSELVES WITH THE CHAMPIONSHIP ATTIRE THAT THEIRS BECAUSE OF WHAT JESUS DID ON THE CROSS.

Secret Power to Winning, Happiness, and a Cool Wardrobe
A Personal Bible Study on the Book of 1 Peter
Susie Shellenberger

RETAIL $9.99
ISBN 0-310-25680-1

invert

Visit www.**invert**books.com or your local bookstore.

Book 1: Nama Beach High
New Girl in Town
Nancy Rue

RETAIL $6.99
ISBN 0-310-24399-8

Book 2: Nama Beach High
False Friends, True Strangers
Nancy Rue

RETAIL $6.99
ISBN 0-310-25180-X

Book 3: Nama Beach High
Fault Lines
Nancy Rue

RETAIL $6.99
ISBN 0-310-25182-6

Book 4: Nama Beach High
Totally Unfair
Nancy Rue

RETAIL $6.99
ISBN 0-310-25183-4

A SERIES OF FICTION FOR TEENAGE GIRLS, THE 'NAMA BEACH HIGH SERIES IS ENGAGING AND ENTERTAINING. BOOKS 1-4 FOLLOW THE LIFE OF LAURA DUFFY AS SHE MOVES TO A NEW SCHOOL, GETS A NEW JOB AND A SECRET ADMIRER. FOLLOW DUFFY ON HER ADVENTURES AS SHE MEETS NEW FRIENDS, AS WELL AS GOD, AND LEARNS WHAT IT'S LIKE TO ADJUST TO A NEW PLACE AND A NEW FAITH.

invert

Visit www.invertbooks.com or your local bookstore.